How to Design, Write, and Present a Successful Dissertation Proposal

For my husband and children,
Patrick, Grace, and Phillip.
For my mother and father,
Gerry and Wayne.

How to Design, Write, and Present a Successful Dissertation Proposal

Elizabeth A. Wentz

Arizona State University

Los Angeles | London | New Delhi
Singapore | Washington DC

Los Angeles | London | New Delhi
Singapore | Washington DC

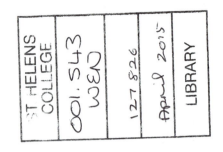
FOR INFORMATION:

SAGE Publications, Inc.

2455 Teller Road

Thousand Oaks, California 91320

E-mail: order@sagepub.com

SAGE Publications Ltd.

1 Oliver's Yard

55 City Road

London EC1Y 1SP

United Kingdom

SAGE Publications India Pvt. Ltd.

B 1/I 1 Mohan Cooperative Industrial Area

Mathura Road, New Delhi 110 044

India

SAGE Publications Asia-Pacific Pte. Ltd.

3 Church Street

#10-04 Samsung Hub

Singapore 049483

Copyright © 2014 by SAGE Publications, Inc.

Printed in the United States of America

Library of Congress Cataloging-in-Publication Data

A catalog record of this book is available from the Library of Congress.

9781452257884

This book is printed on acid-free paper.

Acquisitions Editor: Helen Salmon

Editorial Assistant: Kaitlin Coghill

Production Editor: Brittany Bauhaus

Copy Editor: Mark Bast

Typesetter: C&M Digitals (P) Ltd.

Proofreader: Eleni-Maria Georgiou

Indexer: Rick Hurd

Cover Designer: Karine Hovsepian

Marketing Manager: Nicole Elliott

MIX
Paper from
responsible sources

FSC
www.fsc.org
FSC® C014174

13 14 15 16 17 10 9 8 7 6 5 4 3 2 1

Brief Contents

Detailed Contents

Preface

Graduate school is a journey that will take you places intellectually, physically, and emotionally you have never been before. You will read and learn about things you did not know existed. You will have conversations and debates with faculty and graduate students over interesting problems in the world. You will attend professional conferences and meet leading researchers in your discipline. There will be times of great joy balanced by moments of extreme frustration. You will make friends for life. The goal of this book is to help you start on this journey so that in the end you earn your degree and move toward the next chapter of your life. The journey often starts with designing and writing a research proposal. Therefore, these are the general objectives of this book.

More than likely you already have an idea of a topic to research, but exactly how do you go about turning an idea into a dissertation? Ideas develop from a generalized research concept into specific questions presented as a research proposal (often orally defended). Research proposals provide specificity on what the problem is, why it is important, how others have addressed it, and how you will do it differently. In fact, when you finish the proposal, it may seem as if you have already completed half of the research. This proposal step is essential and required in most PhD programs. Consider the defended proposal a "contract" between you and your committee describing how you aim to solve a specific problem.

This book teaches you specific skills on how to conceptualize, design, and write a successful research proposal. The skills include ethical scientific research, effective reading, and accurate writing. These skills build the foundation to conceptualize a generalized research concept and turn that into specific research questions with methods to support answering those questions.

This book is different from others on writing research proposals because of the activities I advise you to do. During each chapter, I provide short- and medium-length activities that help build the pieces of your research proposal. This is in contrast with other books that provide definitions of sections to write and examples from other students. The tasks, which may not appear fruitful at the time, provide you with the skills to write each section of the proposal. My suggestion at this point, however, is that you should also gather as many books as you can find on how to write in academia, getting through graduate school, writing a research proposal, and finishing your graduate degree. There is no shortage of these books, and each will probably provide a nugget of insight that will move the process along. Find them at used bookstores, online, libraries, your advisor's office, and the shelves of fellow graduate students.

How to Read This Book

To be successful, this book must be read and used. Yes, there are sections meant for reading only. The activities, however, are meant to promote action. These use the philosophy "learn by doing."

1. If you are working on the methods section of your proposal, start by reading and following the writing methods steps in Chapter 11.

2. It is also possible to focus specifically on the activities in the book. The chapter on literature reviews, for example, has detailed activities on extracting both the topics and contributions made by other scholars.

3. And as is the case with most books, reading and working through it from beginning to end is also acceptable.

This text is modeled after several books, including *How to Write A Lot*, by Paul Silvia, which is short, direct, and clear with a lighthearted approach. Likewise, this book contains actions and activities framed in the style of *How to Say It for Women* by Phyllis Mindell and *The Artist's Way* by Julia Cameron to help achieve specific goals. These books, among others, describe writing, speaking, and creative concepts and provide activities that develop skills based on those concepts. Books with this style continue to show that active learning is effective.

Given the independent and group activities, the book could serve as required course reading or to supplement mentoring from an academic advisor. The intended course is one that teaches graduate students how to design and write a research proposal, which is often a required course in a graduate program. The major challenge in the course is to explain by description, activities, and examples how to design and write an informative research proposal. Mentoring styles vary, and students often desire augmented or alternative perspectives on how to perform certain tasks. This book provides such guidance.

My experience as both a mentor and classroom instructor is limited to on-campus doctoral programs and students who primarily use quantitative methods. The activities in this book are focused on students in on-campus social science degree programs, although many can be adapted for distance-learning programs. With creative solutions, such as online teleconference, many of the suggestions can be adapted to students in distance-learning programs. Second, the emphasis of the book is on quantitative methods or mixed methods. Students with research plans involving predominately qualitative methods should seek guidance from the several Sage publications on qualitative research methods.

The graduate students in the Arizona State University course on graduate research design and proposal writing in the School of Geographical Sciences and Urban Planning (GCU 585) inspired me to write this book. In the first years I taught this class, there was no textbook for the course. This frustrated students because they wanted more guidance than what classroom discussion provided. In subsequent years, students used several books that provided background on proposal writing. However, what these books lacked was specific directions on *how to* design and write a research proposal. There was guidance on *what to* include, and there were examples of what that looked like, but there was a large gap between description and delivery. Through many classroom activities, long discussions, and countless student papers, I was motivated to share the detailed steps that helped these students design and write innovative and effective proposals. I am grateful to the feedback these students continue to provide.

Acknowledgments

In addition to the students in the research design and proposal-writing course, this book is the result of the positive influence and support from many people. I would first like to thank Helen Salmon at Sage for taking on this project and always providing me with timely feedback and helpful information and Kaitlin Coghill at SAGE for helping me stay on task. I also want to thank the reviewers for their comments on early drafts of the book: Valerie A. Luzadis, State University of New York College of Environmental Science and Forestry; David L. Brown, Texas A&M University–Commerce; John W. Presley, Illinois State University; Alma Gottlieb, University of Illinois at Urbana–Champaign; and Anne J. Hacker, Walden University. I also appreciate the artistic talent and friendship of Barbara Trapido-Lurie for creating the majority of the figures in the book.

I wish to acknowledge the guidance and patience of my two graduate school mentors: Duane F. Marble and Donna J. Peuquet. Duane, my master's advisor, taught me to always be open to learning. Donna, my PhD advisor, taught me how to dig deeply into a problem and solve problems through innovative solutions. They shared with me their knowledge and gave me fiscal and emotional support to become a teacher and a scholar. In graduate school, I learned as much from my fellow graduate students as I did from my professors. In particular, I am grateful to longtime friends Darlene Wilcox, Harvey Miller, Robin Leichenko, Karen Arabas, and Karen O'Brien for providing inspiration and becoming lifelong friends.

In addition to my graduate school mentors and friends, I also found support and guidance from professors at Arizona State University: Breandán Ó hUallacháin, Pat Gober, and Luc Anselin. They each gave me professional development advice so that I could achieve my own academic and personal goals. The ASU course on research design and proposal writing was often team taught, so I am also in debt to my coinstructors Mike Kuby, Randy Cerveny, and Tony Brazel. In addition to the ASU faculty, I am also grateful for feedback from my own PhD students, including those who finished—Sharolyn Anderson (2002), Darren Ruddell (2009), Won Kyung Kim (2011), and Stephanie Deitrick (2013)—and those in progress—Melinda Shimizu, Yun Ouyang, and Joanna Merson. They are the ultimate test of the methods presented in this book. I thank them for their feedback, their honesty, and their wisdom.

My academic friends are many, and all have heard me talk about writing this book. All of them believed in and encouraged me. I am grateful to Karen Seto, Julia Koschinsky, Jennifer Glick, Ron Dorn, Alan Murray, Serge Rey, Liz Mack, Wenwen Li, Emily Talen, Soe Myint, Bob Balling, Beth Larson, Wei Li, Kevin McHugh, Mike Pasqualetti, Billie Turner, Dan Arreola, Bob Culbertson, Tod Swanson, Scott Yabiku, Kelli Larson, Jana Hutchins, Anne Jones, Volker Benkert, Victor Mesev, Sarah Battersby, Aileen Buckley, Art Getis, Janet Franklin, Will Graf, and Jerry Dobson. My nonacademic friends also encouraged me to write: Michelle Bruckner, Carole Gates, Frank Gates, Becky Ruckman, Mark Hubble, Leila Newsom, Lynn Lintern, and Todd Lintern.

The majority of this book was written while I was on sabbatical as a visiting professor at the Laboratory of Geographic Information Systems (LASIG) at the École Polytechnique Fédérale de Lausanne (EPFL) in Switzerland. The Swiss National Science Foundation provided financial support that made my sabbatical possible. I am grateful to Francois Golay and Stéphane Joost for inviting me to join their research team, and I appreciate the friendship and scholarship of the other members of the LASIG group. I also became good friends with neighbors in Préverenges: Laura Barbieri, Giovanni Boero, Alice Hsy, Marie Claire Cobb, and Krystal and Kelvin Ardister. They made Switzerland my home.

My fortunes run deep as I consider my family who live near and far. Thank you to my family: Pamela Ebert, Gary Ebert, Eric Wentz, Nancy Schwartz, Brenda Conaway, Brigitte Gredt-Vogel, Jörg Vogel, Sarah Valandra, Linda Lentini, JC Valandra, Marisa Valandra, Allen Valandra, and Carrie Valandra.

About the Author

Elizabeth A. Wentz is the associate director for the School of Geographical Sciences and Urban Planning, a professor of geography and planning, and a member of the Executive Committee of the GeoDa Center at Arizona State University. Her research focuses on the design, implementation, and evaluation of geographic technologies with a particular emphasis on applying these tools to study and understand the urban environment. She has authored numerous research articles and book chapters and has served on panels for the National Science Foundation, National Institutes of Health, and other national and international agencies.

1

Introduction

Several times per year throughout the world students fill university stadiums and arenas awaiting the conferral of academic degrees. Each student has at least one thing in common: he or she has successfully fulfilled the requirements for the degree conferred. As a graduate student, you may have sat among the happy bachelorette students, and you may envision your graduate school commencement.

At the commencement ceremony, there is typically a speech or an address given by the university president or a guest speaker. Of course, it contains insights on how to open the next chapter of life and congratulatory remarks to students for their academic accomplishments. There may also be recognition for students who have worked to support their education and appreciation delivered to the people who have supported students along their path to success, such as parents, spouses, and offspring. Faculty members are invited to attend the commencement ceremonies to represent the instruction and guidance the students receive. At the commencement ceremony at my institution, the university president discusses the faculty contribution toward education (central to supporting the success of students). But he also always explains that part of the faculty responsibilities entail *creating new knowledge*. He describes how faculty members are expected to excel in teaching and also in research. As faculty advisors to graduate students, our job is to teach students how to create their own new knowledge. A research proposal is a plan on how to create new knowledge.

The research proposal is often one of the academic requirements to earning a graduate degree. In other words, it is one of the steps you need to complete to attend your graduate commencement. This book offers practical guidance to help you complete the steps of designing, writing, and presenting a research proposal.

The Student Becomes a Scholar

For the first 20+ years of life, each of us was responsible for learning how to navigate and live in this world. Learning is a complex process involving education, training, self-discovery, and experimentation. Through multiple formal processes and informal activities, we demonstrate our mastery of learning. Learning is an active process; therefore, to learn to write a dissertation proposal requires activities. Throughout this book are *Quick Tasks, Action Items,* and *To Do Lists* to support this form of learning.

Formalized demonstration of our learned knowledge includes professional certification, high school degrees, and bachelor of art or science degrees, all publically showing we have mastered particular skills and acquired specific knowledge. Earning these credentials typically involves coursework and other activities.

As an undergraduate student, the primary process toward earning a degree is to demonstrate knowledge in subjects associated with a series of classes. In typical educational settings, demonstrating knowledge occurs through testing—multiple-choice, short-answer, and essay exams. These tests evaluate whether the student understands the subject matter, whether he or she acquired the requisite knowledge. In more advanced classes, instructors sometimes shift the emphasis to comprehension and application. In these cases, evaluation becomes longer essays and class discussion. Graduate school moves these activities a step further.

Graduate school expects that students are more than just *knowledgeable* about a subject area but rather are *masters* of the subject matter and *leaders* in the field. Mastery of a subject means an individual has a significantly deeper focus and understanding of a particular subject. Leadership takes mastery one more step by indicating more than expertise. Leadership indicates that as a master of a subject, he or she is influential in moving knowledge forward. Moving knowledge forward means creating new knowledge.

The expectation of creating new knowledge is the primary distinction between undergraduate and graduate students. Creating new knowledge means understanding something not understood before. The research proposal describes how that new knowledge will be created.

The research proposal defines a research trajectory. A trajectory is a path through space and time under the influence of external forces. In an academic context, the trajectory is a path consisting of research areas and problems solved under the influence of external forces such as collaborators, data availability, funding opportunities, and new knowledge. The trajectory analogy suggests, too, a logical connection from one research phase to the next. This process of encountering problems and producing solutions evolves over time. The trajectory starts with a foundation and extends beyond it from your experiences, activities, expertise, and interests.

The PhD graduate advisor is part of the foundation in forming a student's own research trajectory. A "foundation" in construction terminology refers to the lowest and supporting layer that stabilizes or grounds a building to the surface of the earth. By extension, the foundation of a research trajectory is the base and starting point that grounds research to the academic community. Like the construction analogy, the research foundation supports future work but does not necessarily define it. A concrete building foundation does not necessarily mean the structure itself is made of concrete, and just because your PhD advisor is world-renown for a specific qualitative method does not mean that method will become your specialty as well.

The connectivity of the research trajectory is often more visible upon reflection. It is then possible to see the train of thought, the influence of external forces, and the new knowledge acquired from one research phase to the next. However, to move forward, academics need to have a plan or research agenda. These plans consist of developing a written document that describes 5 or 10 years of activities to attain specific research objectives. For graduate students, these plans (consisting in part of the dissertation proposal) are generally designed to prepare students for the job market and look 3 to 5 years into the future. Your academic advisor can guide you through developing the plan and executing it. Select an advisor that matches your professional and personal expectations.

 Action Item

Look at the current jobs announcements in your discipline. Examine the subfields and expectations. Consider that in 3 to 5 years, there will be similar job announcements. What do you need to do between now and then to be competitive for these positions?

Importance of a Research Proposal

A research proposal describes in detail the research you will do. It describes the problem (or the area of unknown knowledge) you aim to address, why it is important, what others have done in this area, and how you plan to do something unique. In other words, the proposal describes your *plan* for *creating new knowledge.* The proposal also describes the activities you will do to earn a graduate degree. Research proposals vary considerably in their length and level of detail. The depth and length depend on the norms in your own discipline, the tradition within your academic unit, and the guidance provided by your advisor and committee. The level of detail can be simply a rough sketch of your ideas, a simple or detailed outline of your dissertation, detailed descriptions of your exact experiments, or even preliminary results from a pilot study. Likewise, the length of the document can range from a few pages to a hundred or more pages.

In most universities, you are required to present formally the dissertation prospectus, and in some cases, it is considered a defense. Once approved by your committee, the proposal becomes a contract between you and your committee indicating what you will do to fulfill this part of your requirement for earning your degree. You are saying to the committee, "This is the unknown knowledge I have identified, and this is how I intend to learn more about it." The committee's responsibility is to evaluate the plan and make sure there is enough substance in your proposal to constitute a contribution to knowledge generation. Similarly, the committee needs to be sure the research plan is not too large and therefore unreasonable for you to complete.

The contract works both ways. It also is a description of the "end" of your dissertation research. In other words, if you have completed the tasks stated in your proposal, the committee or your advisor should not come back to you and say, "Well, this research really needs a bit more here and a bit more there to be complete." If those new "bits and pieces" are not part of your proposal (which you can view as a contract), then you are able to tell the committee you have fulfilled the research requirements as stated in your proposal (and signed by your committee) and these new suggestions are excellent ideas for future research. The beauty of a good dissertation topic is it will inevitably open up new avenues of research. It is not your obligation to complete all new avenues as part of your dissertation research.

Hence, the proposal places the necessary boundaries on this phase of the research for both you and your committee. It is critical to get it right because it sets the tone for the kind of research you will do.

Common pitfalls in writing a dissertation proposal include the following:

- Not knowing the literature well enough to develop a meaningful research question
- Spending too much time on the literature review (not knowing when to stop reviewing and begin researching)
- Providing scant details on the research plan; thinking that a little hand waving or a statement about how the methods will be decided as the research unfolds is sufficient
- Poorly articulating the theoretical framework of the research
- Not understanding the relevance of the research as a contribution of knowledge
- Not understanding that writing a dissertation proposal is not a 1-week (or even a 1-month) effort

This book helps avoid these pitfalls.

The Book's Plan

The first paragraphs of this chapter describe a goal—attending a graduation ceremony. To achieve that goal, several milestones need to be met, including designing, writing, and defending a research proposal. This book provides practical guidance on how to develop a specific research plan from a generalized idea to a specifically defined written document and oral presentation. Figure 1.1 illustrates a spiral. The top of the spiral represents the general subject matter that interests you. The bottom of the spiral represents the specific research problem you will solve in your dissertation. The chapters in this book describe how to move from the top of the spiral to the bottom.

Figure 1.1   The research spiral illustrates the path from a general
research interest to a specific research problem.

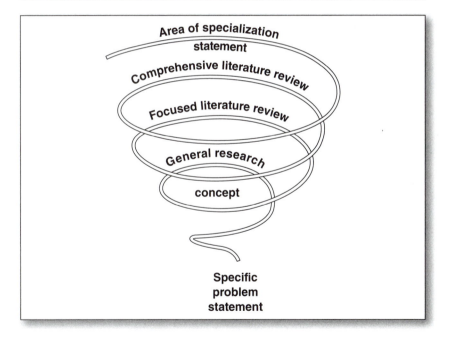

The 14 chapters of this book are designed to guide graduate students and advanced undergraduate students through the process of designing a research plan and writing ideas into a comprehensive proposal. The book provides a balance between descriptions of proposal sections, specific tasks and activities to design and write each section, and guidance on dealing with the emotional pitfalls many students face.

Chapter 2 begins with important comments on academic integrity. It clarifies what is acceptable research practice and what is not. More often than not, students first encounter academic integrity in the classroom. Students are expected to complete their own work and not copy that of others. Scholarly ethics, however, extend beyond cheating. Chapter 2 provides descriptions of several ethical topics and scenarios for how to handle them.

Chapter 3 describes how to begin a research trajectory with a curriculum vitae (CV). The trajectory that aims for a research proposal and beyond begins by evaluating the past and how it forms a basis for the path forward. This chapter describes the CV and how to write one. While the CV documents the past professional record, it is also a vital tool throughout an academic career. It provides examiners with explicit and detailed knowledge of a scholar's skills. While a proposal is forward looking, the CV is backward looking and a pivot for defining a scholar's research trajectory.

A short description of a scholar's area of specialization (AOS) bridges the past (the CV) with the future (the research proposal). Chapter 4 describes what an area-of-specialization statement is, why it is important, and how to write an effective one. The AOS defines the subdiscipline that will become the focus of research, identifies the research problems within that subdiscipline, and explains the skills needed to accomplish research in that subdiscipline.

The next two chapters of the book describe important skills for graduate students: effective reading (Chapter 5) and writing (Chapter 6). Graduate-level skills in reading require effectiveness, which means being able to read broadly and conceptualize the big picture as well as knowing the details of certain studies. Broad and detailed reading must be accomplished efficiently because there is so much literature to synthesize. Chapter 6 provides guidance to graduate students on how to explain their ideas through writing. The writing chapter covers many of the topics that emphasize and build on the writing skills learned as an undergraduate.

Building on the topics of the AOS statement (Chapter 4) and the reading (Chapter 5) and writing (Chapter 6) skills just identified, the literature review (Chapter 7) is an essential next step to the research proposal. The literature review synthesizes the existing literature by describing what has been studied, what was found, and how the findings relate to gaps in knowledge. While this step is essential, students can become bogged down in details or miss entire portions of the literature. Chapter 7 provides practical steps on how to effectively and efficiently stay up to date on the literature. It explains how to differentiate between a summary of the literature and a critical, synthetic analysis of the literature.

Chapter 8 provides a break from the steps of writing a research proposal to describe the role of the academic advisor and the remainder of the support system in the academic village. The academic advisor is typically the most important person in the proposal writing process. Different styles, expectations, and responsibilities of both the student and the advisor are described. By the time you own and read this book, you probably already have an academic advisor, but it is important to coordinate with your advisor on the kind of interaction you both expect during the proposal writing step and then the research. Some students are highly independent and desire more autonomy than others. Some professors expect that level of autonomy. Other students and advisors work more closely together. Chapter 8 also describes the role that other academic partners play in the process of earning a degree. It explains styles, expectations, and responsibilities of the academic village.

Returning to the steps in writing a dissertation proposal, the next two chapters describe how to conceptualize a generalized research concept (Chapter 9) and how to turn the ideas into a specific research question or objective (Chapter 10). Chapter 9 describes how to identify a generalized research concept. This is a description of a knowledge gap in the literature that your research aims to address. It is less specific than a research question and more specific than the overarching literature review. Chapter 10 describes how to write a problem statement, a specific instance of the generalized research concept. This section of the proposal identifies the research question or objective and the rationale for why it fills a gap in knowledge.

Chapter 11 describes what is required for deciding on and writing about the research methods. Research methods are activities an investigator performs to answer the research questions or meet the research objectives. Two approaches for writing the research methods are described. The first is a standard approach, and the second reflects how to approach methods when the research has a theoretical or methodological approach. The standard approach involves describing the study area, data sources, and analysis. Theoretical or methodological research methods describe the generic framework followed by an approach to evaluate the new method or theory.

There are two culminating tangible outcomes from this book: a written research proposal (Chapter 12) and an oral presentation of the proposal (Chapter 13). The written research proposal describes the research problem, why it is important, how the problem has been addressed or unstudied before, and how the current project aims to solve the problem. It is the result of the activities written about in previous chapters. The chapter describes how to assemble pieces already written and organize them into a single document.

Complementary to the written document is an oral presentation of the research proposal. More often than not, little attention is given to how to present effectively. Chapter 13 provides practical guidance on content (what to include as well as what to exclude), organization (what order and level of detail for each section), and presentation (visual aids and speaking style). The emphasis is to eliminate or minimize reliance on text-based slides so the speaker is more engaged with the audience. This chapter describes how to prepare and deliver a high-quality presentation.

The proposal is clearly an important accomplishment toward earning a graduate degree. There is certainly time to celebrate this important milestone. However, the research plans just described need to be implemented. The last chapter of the book (Chapter 14) describes how to assimilate the learning experiences from writing the proposal to move forward and complete the degree. The content of this chapter includes how to reuse portions of the text, how to use the time line effectively, how to engage in the review process, and how to overcome common struggles.

Audience

The audience for this book is students in doctoral programs in the social and behavioral sciences with research plans that use primarily quantitative methods. Most of the references are toward doctoral programs, but many of the ideas can be extended to students writing proposals for master's theses or undergraduate honors papers. It is assumed that the students are in residence so that there are face-to-face interactions with faculty and other graduate students. That said, many of the Action Items can be adapted to distance learners (e.g., online video conferences in place of in-person meetings), and many of the Action Items are done alone. The format of the proposal, including the research questions, methods, and structure of the document, leans toward students with quantitative or mixed quantitative/ qualitative research plans. While there is some attention to qualitative methods, it is not the focus.

Motivation

I designed this book to be actively read (see Chapter 5 for a discussion on active versus passive reading). Throughout the book are Action Items, which describe activities the reader should complete to conclude "reading" this book with a successful research proposal in hand. Throughout the book there are activities that support development of a research proposal. Those listed as *Quick Tasks* take only a few minutes. *Action Items* will take a day or so to finish. *To Do Lists* are substantial activities and will require several days or weeks to complete.

Students have asked me how long it takes to write and defend a research proposal. The activities described in this book require about 3 to 4 months for the typical student in the social sciences to complete. This rule of thumb however is discipline, department, advisor, and student specific. Often unique circumstances lead to a longer or shorter amount of time to design and write a proposal. Regardless of the time required, staying focused and working each day results in progress toward the degree.

Staying focused and motivated often requires some external help. As researchers pushing past the boundaries of known knowledge, adversities (such as rejection, setbacks) are normal. In fact, they are expected. They are nevertheless difficult. The key to success in academia is to move beyond these struggles and become stronger and wiser as a result. I have found that slogans, sayings, expressions, proverbs, and general words of wisdom help me overcome the emotional anger and frustration with such adversities. They help me remember that I am not alone in the struggle and that I can continue to work. Some common motivational expressions include these:

If at first you don't succeed, try, try again.

Don't throw the baby out with the bathwater.

"We are what we repeatedly do. Excellence, therefore, is not an act but a habit."—Aristotle

"Men's best successes come after their disappointments."—Henry Ward Beecher

"Genius is 1% inspiration and 99% perspiration."—Thomas Edison

In addition to inspirational sayings, photos and images can also provide powerful inspiration. One I use comes to mind. It is a photo from a magazine of a person carrying a mountain bike through deep, deep snow. The determination of this person despite the clear adversity was an inspiration to me (plus my passion for cycling contributed to my interest in the image). Creating new knowledge is difficult and occasionally not fun. Success requires determination sometimes derived from unusual sources.

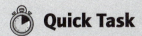

Quick Task

Select a slogan or an image that inspires you to keep working even through adversity. Put it in a place where you can see it when you need it—at your desk, digitally on your desktop, or inside your medicine cabinet next to your toothbrush.

Reminders

- Graduate students are creators of new knowledge.
- Be a leader.
- The dissertation proposal is a contract.
- Visualize a trajectory.
- Stay strong, stay motivated.

2

Ethics

Introduction

Imagine this scenario. One of your fellow graduate students is writing her dissertation proposal and plans to defend it in about 3 months. Her advisor suggests to her that she look at other proposals that were successfully defended. She turns to you and asks to see your dissertation prospectus that you defended this past fall. You hesitate. It sounds possible that you might have similar topics. You are concerned because you put a lot of work into compiling the literature, determining the key points in the literature, framing your research question, and writing your methods. What do you do? Is it possible that she could take your ideas? Should you share the proposal and hope she understands that this is your work?

The answer is yes; you should willingly give her the copy of your proposal. To begin with, at most universities, the dissertation prospectus is public record. So even if you do not give it to her, she does have a right to see it. Second, if she behaves in an unethical manner by plagiarizing your work, then she could fail her proposal defense or, worse, be dismissed from the university without her degree. If you are seriously concerned, then you are obliged to follow up by reading her proposal and attending her defense.

Concerns such as this are an example of the importance of academic integrity. This chapter describes the importance and role of academic integrity and how to identify and avoid unethical behavior. Professional reputation, collaborative research, scientific misconduct, human subject testing, harassment, and work-life balance are covered. These topics broadly explore how you expect to be treated and how you should treat others. Many situations are clear. Others are not, particularly when they involve someone of authority.

The Scientist as Autonomous Being

How to write your curriculum vitae (CV) is covered in Chapter 3. A CV is a document that describes the scholarship and academic activities of an individual, including degrees earned, positions held, papers published, and grants awarded. Professionals in research perform their work in a university as a professor or at a government or nongovernment agency as a research scholar. There is a mutual benefit for both the scholar and the institution with this association. For the scholar, a reputable university or research agency adds prestige to his or her career. It suggests the scholar meets a certain standards of academic and professional excellence. Practically, it also means resources to support the scholar's research, in space, money, and personnel. There is also the potential for top-notch colleagues, including the best graduate students and postdocs.

For the university or research agency, the institution's reputation improves with the productivity and reputation of the scholar. Each scholar is an investment with an anticipated return on the investment. The fiscal return comes from the grants and students, where each brings revenue to the university or agency. The nonmonetary returns are found in the local, national, and international reputation by bringing positive press about the university or agency.

For the institution, the positive, win-win relationship, however, only goes so far. The scholar remains an autonomous entity. Academic scholars who move to a different institution take their reputation, and potentially their postdocs, students, and grant money, with them. Given this status as an autonomous being, a critical component to remember is that your name is your legacy. You build your legacy with your behavior, your collaboration with colleagues, and the quality of the scholarship you produce.

Collaborative Research

Researchers who work independently 100% of the time are rare. More frequently, scholars work collaboratively with colleagues, postdocs, and graduate and undergraduate students. Collaborative research suggests that the whole is worth more than the sum of the parts. Collaborators each bring different experience, skills, and expertise to the table. Furthermore, in an era of multi-, cross-, and transdisciplinary research initiatives, collaborations are extending beyond the colleagues down the hall. Collaborative research demands trust.

Trust refers to an expectation or reliance on another person to perform the work expected in a timely, accurate, and ethical manner. *Timely* means you will deliver your part of the research when you agreed to do it. Potentially extenuating circumstances sometimes prevent on-time delivery, but these should be rare. When these do occur, it is your obligation to communicate with the project leader as soon as possible to minimize the impact on the rest of the project. *Accurate* means you need to check your work. If you are analyzing data, proof your work, examine the results critically, and ask yourself if the results make sense or not. Use common sense and avoid assuming that since the computer generated the results, all is fine. If you are preparing a bibliography or literature summary, check for accuracy in the references. There is no excuse for incorrect article titles, misspelled author names, missing page numbers, or incorrect formatting. These seemingly minor issues point to a larger problem—carelessness. Seeing carelessness in a bibliography suggests this problem may extend into other parts of the research that are harder to detect.

Finally, collaborative researchers expect the work to be performed ethically. Ethical research extends into many areas but includes falsifying data, manipulating results, and plagiarizing words (further discussed in the Scientific Misconduct section that follows). The implications of scientific misconduct impact the reputation of *everyone* involved from the institution to the individuals.

While everyone is blamed when research is performed unethically, individuals also deserve due credit for high-quality, publishable research. In collaborative research, anyone who participates should receive credit for his or her contribution. Credit for work ranges from being an author on a referred paper to being named in the acknowledgments. In some fields, the principal author—who receives the most recognition for the manuscript—is the last author. In other fields, the first author receives the most recognition. This person is also the one who has the most responsibility, including correspondence with the editor and being the contact person listed on the paper after it is published.

The key for deciding who should be the principal author comes from communication. Talk to your advisor about who should be included and in what order. Some advisors require coauthorship (and even principal authorship) on all student manuscripts. Other advisors are more relaxed about their expectations. Speak to your advisor as you are preparing a manuscript about who should be included on a paper and in what order.

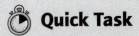

Quick Task

Speak with your advisor about the norms and expectations on authorship in your discipline and specifically with him or her.

Scientific Misconduct

Scientific misconduct is any aspect of unethical, untruthful, or deceitful action performed during the pursuit of greater knowledge, regardless of whether the work is collaborative. Scientific misconduct of any form will permanently damage your reputation and perhaps those of your colleagues. Slandering a colleague, stealing ideas, collecting data unethically, falsifying data, manipulating results, and plagiarizing words or images can lead to a damaged career. Actions that may not seem like a big deal at the time, such as a quick copy and paste from a website or a small change to a few data values, are a big deal.

Most forms of scientific misconduct are conscious and deliberate, deliberate "fudges" to improve an outcome. These actions are taken instead of the ethical path because of unsatisfactory results, looming deadlines, external pressure to succeed, and lack of understanding of scientific misconduct. Some forms of scientific misconduct arise unintentionally due to carelessness or inattentiveness in any aspect of the research, from reviewing the literature, to collecting data, to analyzing data, to interpreting results, to writing. None of these reasons—even sloppiness or naïveté—satisfactorily excuse scientific misconduct, nor do they reduce the impact on one's career.

SLANDER

Deliberately damaging a colleague's reputation and potentially his or her career is morally wrong. Examples of deliberate actions that can damage another person's career are the following:

- A professor can slow down or prevent a student from earning a degree or write damaging recommendation letters during a job search.
- A colleague can discourage someone from pursuing a good idea and then later use that idea himself or herself.
- A reviewer can write an unfair review for a submitted manuscript or proposal.
- A senior scholar can write a negative letter for a junior scholar, ultimately preventing the person from being promoted.
- An administrator can reject a person from promotion for undocumented or undisclosed reasons.
- Anyone who uses slander against another in a public or private setting can permanently damage the reputation of another individual.

Why do people do these things? There are myriad reasons, but most often the target is someone seen as a threat to the perpetrator's success, such as an intelligent and productive junior scholar who threatens the norms. Victims can sometimes find legal recourse, but the damage to their career can be permanent regardless of the outcome of a lawsuit. If you are discovered to be the perpetrator, your reputation as a professional is also then damaged. Avoid such situations through honesty.

If you are ever a victim of slander you need to pursue it through the appropriate channels. Start by investigating the options within your institution. If the situation is extremely serious, seek legal counsel.

STEALING IDEAS

A critical element of scholarship is reviewing and providing feedback on the work of others. Feedback is provided to students by professors and to scholars for manuscripts submitted to journals and for proposals submitted to granting agencies. More information on how to effectively give informative feedback is provided in Chapter 14. A potential ethical issue in this process is that reviewers are experts in the subject matter and are also investigating similar subjects. This means reviewers have the potential to learn from and potentially steal from another person's work. While it is impossible to read someone's work and not learn from it, the ethical action is to not steal anyone else's ideas from this process.

Some of the ideas being developed by colleagues are no doubt excellent, and the temptation to use these ideas may be high. But remember, each scholar is an autonomous entity, and using these ideas is stealing. The outcome does not result in a new television or cash in hand, because the goods are intellectual property. But when discovered, the damage to your reputation is permanent.

If you find yourself a victim, you need to speak immediately with your advisor or program director about the proper course of action. The course of action will vary depending on the nature of the infraction, who is involved, and the institutional support. Unfortunately, depending on the situation, there may be little you can do. Too many situations have shown this to be the case. The only bright side is that if you had one good idea, then you will likely come up with another and another.

PLAGIARISM

Plagiarism is a specific form of stealing ideas. It involves using the words or ideas from another without identifying the source. In other words, if you plagiarize, you are attempting to represent someone else's work as your own. Digital resources and the copy/paste functions make note taking easy. However, being sloppy in this exercise by forgetting to reference sources makes anyone vulnerable.

Intentional or not, plagiarism is unethical. For example, students have said to me, "I meant to go back and add citations when I was done." These students are suggesting that they unintentionally copied ideas from another paper. However, plagiarism is the intentional *or unintentional* use of another person's ideas and words in an effort to represent them as their own. Being sloppy or ignorant is not an excuse.

Instructors have turned to software to evaluate student papers. The software identifies the probability of plagiarism by comparing a paper to published sources. Similarly, a quick search on Google with key phrases often identifies the original source of a phrase or paragraph, which places a student or anyone in a precarious academic position.

FALSIFYING DATA AND RESULTS

Falsifying data means deliberately adding or manipulating data to obtain the desired results. While it can be accidental (e.g., incorrectly converting data from one set of units into another), more often than not, data falsification is intentional. Falsified data have been manipulated to support a particular hypothesis.

Unethical research propagates errors. This means that published research with fudged results will become the basis of future research by other scholars. The problems are compounded as more research is built upon this faulty work. If the foundation upon which you build your own research is unstable, then your research crumbles too. In the best-case scenario, the problem is uncovered and no future work is jeopardized. In these cases, only the researchers are penalized (jobs are lost, reputations are damaged, and careers end). In the worst-case scenario, falsified research results are used in national or local decision making, public policy formation, health care policy, or pharmaceuticals. In these cases, potentially many people in the private and public sectors are hurt because the outcomes differ from what was expected.

Problems associated with scholarship are discovered in several ways, such as a simple Internet search. Problems appear also when another lab or research group attempts to reproduce your work. For example, say your paper applies a new method for analysis, showing satisfactory results. The other research group is unable to obtain the same level of results because you adjusted your results a bit. This is problematic because research is built on the knowledge and experience of others.

⏱ To Do List

1. Be knowledgeable. Search for information on ethical conduct in research. One example is an interactive video produced by the Office of Research Integrity in the U.S. Health and Human Services. By role-playing as different members of the university, this online video illustrates the responsibility of members of a research team when potentially faced with questions of scientific misconduct. It provides excellent insight into the

opportunities individuals have to act one way or another and the potential outcome of these choices. The video can be viewed at the following website: http://ori.hhs.gov/thelab.

2. Don't be sloppy; get organized. If you are inherently a neat and organized person, then, great, you are set. Otherwise, make a promise with yourself to become neater—at least with your work projects. Here are some starting points:

- Recognize and agree to the fact that being organized takes time and plan "organizing my stuff" into your activities.
- Have a dedicated workspace (or two). At home, the workspace needs to be something more than a portion of the kitchen table, even if it means stuffing a desk into a closet (that was my home office in graduate school).
- Organize computer files into folders; separate work activities from personal ones.
- Have a backup system in place. Invest in an external hard drive or in cloud space and back up your files on a regular basis.
- If you are hopelessly lost, dedicate yourself to improving your organizational skills. Find online resources or books to help get organized. Find a system that works for you.

Human Subject Testing

Research requiring data on human activities, opinions, feelings, and biological response is central to the social and behavioral sciences. Consequently, investigators must know their responsibilities to protect the rights and welfare of their subjects. Vulnerable populations such as children, the elderly, the incarcerated, and the mentally and/or physically impaired are given particularly close attention because they may not understand the implications of the investigation. Some of the rights and welfare of the subjects include the following:

- The right to protect their identity
- The right to withdraw from the investigation, regardless of whether the data collection is complete
- The right to know how the data will be used
- The right to know that data collected are used in the way they were promised and in no other way
- The right to know the risks associated with the testing and data collection
- The right to not be exposed to unnecessary harm

To ensure these and other rights are not violated, investigators who acquire data on humans are required to have their research plan approved by a review board, often call the Institutional Review Board, or IRB. Prior to submitting a research plan to the IRB, investigators are required to complete a training certificate. Earning the training certificate requires taking a short course and passing a test, which are available online. The training certificate indicates one is knowledgeable about human subject testing.

 Action Item

Search for the research integrity office at your institution. Read the IRB requirements for obtaining permission to use human subjects in research. If you expect your research to involve human subjects, begin to take the required seminars and tests.

At most universities and institutions the IRB meets at regular intervals to review applications. IRB applications can require a full review (which can take several months to gain approval), exempt status (because the research falls within certain typical categories such as an educational setting), or an expedited review (in which the study falls under certain categories). The process to gain approval is clearly outlined and typically involves training (described earlier) and submitting an application. The application includes, among other items, a detailed description of the study and explicit details on how data will be collected and used.

Studies involving animal testing have rules as well. Animal testing appears less often in the social and behavior sciences. Nevertheless, like human subject testing rules, these rules are to protect the rights and welfare of animals. If you expect your research to include animals, learn about investigator responsibilities in animal subject testing.

Harassment

Harassment is any type of bullying a person uses against another, typically to assert power, dominance, or control. It could be unfavorable comments directed at an individual, inappropriate discussions behind someone's back, or direct threats to someone with the suggestion of serious ramifications. The result can be an uncomfortable or even hostile work environment.

Like harassment generally, sexual harassment is any form of unwelcome sexual advance. Some assume that the harasser is always male and the victim is always female. That is not the case. Sexual harassment can be any combination of male or female harasser and victim. Furthermore, the harassment may not always be directed from a professor toward a student (although that is more often the case). Any combination is possible. Sexual harassment can be as subtle as inappropriate comments or as direct as threats. More direct threats of sexual assault are also illegal.

Most instances of harassment have a difficult path toward resolution. If you are a victim of harassment or sexual harassment or you know someone who is, seek help. All universities have an office where you can go and speak to someone confidentially about a situation. They can help you decide how to proceed.

In contrast to harassment are consensual relationships with co-workers. The only real ethical issue occurs when one is a minor or one is in a decision-making position over the other. A decision-making role involves assigning grades, determining passing a class, or signing off on a degree. If this is the case, then both parties are at risk. If you are a teaching assistant (TA), do not ask to date anyone in your class. Instead, make the advance *after* the end of the semester. Likewise, if you are a graduate student interested in a professor, do not take classes from that person or have him or her serve on your committee. Situations do occur where professors and graduate students have dated, and some are now happily married couples. In these cases, the professors and the students made conscious choices to wait until the end of the semester, to drop a class that was being taken, or to never enter a situation where one had authority over the other.

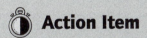 **Action Item**

Read your university's policies on harassment. Educate yourself on what actions are inappropriate and the procedures outlined to resolve them. Do not assume you will not need these resources.

Enjoying Life

Graduate school can feel as if you are hurtling yourself from one deadline to the next through finishing coursework, comprehensive exams, grant deadlines, and defending a dissertation. It is tempting to wait until the list is "done" to go out and have some fun. Unfortunately, if one waits until the list is done, stress and anxiety will become a norm. Furthermore, using that model will result in a person who waits to have fun until a tenured full professor. By then, the pattern of all work and no play will be established.

Mental and emotional health experts describe the importance of fun and free time and how it is positively related to productivity. This means you should incorporate "free time" into your schedule now so that you maximize your productivity. Leisure activities can be time alone or with friends or family. This emphasizes doing the things you enjoy. Some examples include these:

- Cooking
- Shopping
- Exercising (biking, walking, hiking, weight lifting, paddling)
- Playing music
- Playing cards or board games
- Watching television or movies
- Reading novels
- Traveling
- Painting
- Going to museums or cultural sites

Build extracurricular activities into your work life now.

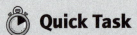 **Quick Task**

Work fun into your regular schedule. Graduate school is a busy time, but make time for your personal life too.

Reminders

- The scientist is an autonomous being.
- Enter into the review process with respect.
- Take seriously any concerns or questions over scientific misconduct.
- Harassment is any form of bullying from subtle to direct.
- Make time for fun in your life.

3

Curriculum Vitae

Introduction

The first two chapters described the need to generate a research trajectory and how to do so. The foundation for the research trajectory is the curriculum vitae (CV). The CV documents all professional activities—describing the professional path so far—and inferring the future trajectory. Therefore, to start a research proposal, begin with what is already done. Build the foundation. This chapter describes how to write, revise, and maintain a CV that effectively describes your academic past and sets the stage for presenting your academic future.

There are two reasons to write about past activities when starting to write about the future. The first reason is, as stated previously, because your CV describes a research trajectory. The CV places your past on a path that lines up with what you plan to do in the future. Initially this can be a tool for you (Who am I? and Why am I here?), but it is an important tool for other readers too. It is incumbent on you to make the linkage between the past and the future. This is the only piece of the proposal that looks backward—everything else is forward looking.

The second reason is practical. First, many grant applications (e.g., a research proposal, which is what you are writing here), require—at the very least—an abbreviated CV. The CV shows that the principle investigators (PIs) are qualified to do the work proposed. The grant proposal reviewers examine the CV as part of a proposal to determine if the investigators have the skills to execute the research proposed. They want insight on whether the investigators have the ability to collect data, write software, analyze results, and produce journal articles, as stated in the proposal.

Forms of the CV

The CV (also known as an academic vitae) is a dynamic document that details your professional academic record. The word *vitae* is derived from a

Latin word meaning "life," indicating a tool to describe your life (and one you will use throughout your life). The word *curriculum* means "a course of action" and is often used in reference to a plan of study toward earning a degree. A curriculum vitae does not necessarily describe a plan, which is why the term *academic vitae* is sometimes used in its place. Instead the curriculum vitae describes your past academic course of action. The term you use may be discipline or university dependent. I use the term curriculum vitae, or CV, in this book.

Some define the CV as a brief summary of professional accomplishments or as the equivalent to a résumé. The CV and résumé are both comprehensive documents. The difference is the level of detail used to make the document complete. A CV is a detailed record of all professional accomplishments. A professional résumé highlights or references one's professional accomplishments. Both are comprehensive, but the level of detail describing the accomplishments is different.

The word *résumé* translates from French to mean "summary," implying a brief but comprehensive record. Some recommendations suggest a résumé should be one page for professionals with a bachelor's degree or less than 10 years of experience. Professionals with a master's degree or more than 10 years of experience can have a résumé of 2 pages or slightly longer. The idea behind the shorter résumé (particularly compared to the CV) is that busy executives or HR personnel will spend only a few seconds glancing at the document; therefore to capture his or her attention, you need a document that immediately shows key accomplishments. Since the résumé is concise, it highlights key points along the career (making it comprehensive), but it does not need to cover every detail of the path. Some academics maintain a résumé for consultancy and other professional purposes along with a CV for academic purposes.

An abbreviated CV (sometimes called a biosketch) is also different from a professional résumé. An abbreviated CV is not comprehensive. It covers the most recent record or relevant record for the task at hand. An abbreviated CV is sometimes incorporated in professional websites, showing only recent work. An abbreviated CV is often required for grant applications, showing only work related to the grant application. Therefore it might be quite detailed in some areas (e.g., publications directly related to the specific application) and brief or nonexistent in others (e.g., unrelated publications). Some granting agencies (e.g., the National Science Foundation) provide specific instructions on the content, organization, and length of the abbreviated CV. They are even specific on the number of publications you are allowed to include (current guidelines from the NSF request five publications most related to the proposed research and five other publications).

A CV has a number of uses throughout your career. It can be required with a dissertation document. You will need a CV (and a cover letter, but that is not part of this discussion) to apply for an academic position—a postdoctoral or tenure-track faculty position. As already mentioned, your complete CV or an abbreviated CV will be needed for most grant applications. Later, your CV will be included in your promotion materials. If you are asked to serve as a committee member for a student in a different institution, you may be asked for a copy of your CV to approve your inclusion in the committee. A CV is used any time knowledge of past accomplishments is needed. It is therefore critical that the content is up to date, accurate, and thorough at all times.

Content

There are different opinions on what to include and exclude from a CV. In the end, the choice is essentially discipline specific and personal. Most disciplines expect you to list your degrees earned, employment record, publications (preferably differentiated between referred and nonreferred), and grant history. Certain disciplines expect awards, courses taught, students mentored, and professional service.

Your first CV will probably be relatively short (maybe even less than one page). I use the CV as an assignment in the research design and proposal writing class I teach. Students sometimes ask if I grade on the content—e.g., the number of publications (or lack of them). The list of accomplishments is not important. What is important is that you have started and are thinking about it relative to a research trajectory.

As important as it is to remember what to include, there are also past activities you should exclude. Do not include nonprofessional employment such as your summer job at McDonalds (or your current job at Chili's). Include past employment when it is part of your professional training (e.g., if your graduate program is in restaurant management, then these jobs might be relevant).

The difficult decision on what to include and exclude occurs in cases where a person has made a moderate or radical career change. Some students have started a PhD after a lengthy professional career in a different field. They need to decide how much detail about their prior profession to keep on record. In these cases, some indication of past activities should be included, job titles at the very least. What to avoid is gaps—particularly large ones—in the record. Sometimes large gaps are unavoidable because of illness, parenting responsibilities (e.g., stay-at-home parents returning to school), or other personal reasons. These cases make it harder to provide a complete record. It is therefore incumbent on you to explain the gap in a cover letter or other form of supporting material.

Personal information can be included or excluded. Common examples include volunteer or nonacademic interests such as hiking, cooking, time with family, and speaking foreign languages. At one point, including one's social security number was common practice, but you should *exclude* it to protect your fiscal identity. When adding personal information to the CV avoid including a long list, but a short piece adds character and interest to a comprehensive CV.

Style

Consistency. After content, this is the most important consideration. The style of the CV refers to font type, font size, indentation, spacing between items, referencing style—everything about the way your CV looks. In particular, consistency applies to the chronological order in which you present your work. Some people (perhaps in response to their discipline) list their most recent work first. Others list their work from oldest to newest.

Recently I undertook the task of reformatting my CV into a new style. In my old style, the year of my accomplishments was buried in the description of each item (see Figure 3.1). It was difficult to follow the lineage of my work over

Figure 3.1   This CV style emphasizes author names.

Koerner, Brenda, **Elizabeth A. Wentz**, and Robert Balling, Jr. 2004. Projected carbon dioxide (CO_2) for the year 2020 in Phoenix, Arizona. *Environmental Management* 33 Supplement: S222–S228.

Miller, Harvey and **Elizabeth A. Wentz** 2003. Geographic representation in geographic information systems and spatial analysis. *Annals of the Association of American Geographers* 93(3): 574–594.

Wentz, Elizabeth A., Aimee F. Campbell, and Robert Houston 2003. Implementing and testing two methods of spatio-temporal data interpolation applied to tracking the movement of monkeys. *International Journal of Geographical Information Science* 17(7): 623–645.

Day, Thomas A., Patricia Gober, Fusheng S. Xiong, and **Elizabeth A. Wentz** 2002. Temporal patterns in near-surface CO2 concentrations over contrasting vegetation types in the Phoenix metropolitan area. *Agricultural and Forest Meteorology* 110(3): 229–245.

> **Wentz, Elizabeth A.**, Patricia Gober, Robert C. Balling, Jr., and Thomas Day 2002. Spatial patterns and determinants of carbon dioxide in an urban environment. *The Annals of the Association of American Geographers* 92(1): 15–28.

several pages. In the new style, I continued to list my work in reverse chronological order, but I left justified the year so the lineage could be clearly followed. I also changed the font, eliminated the bold font in my name, and removed the spaces between the article references (see Figure 3.2).

Figure 3.1 shows an earlier style of my CV. The publication year is embedded in the reference, and therefore it is difficult to follow the chronology. My name is highlighted however to bring out my role in coauthored publications.

Figure 3.2   This CV style emphasizes publication year.

2004	Koerner, Brenda, Elizabeth A. Wentz, and Robert Balling, Jr. 2004. Projected carbon dioxide (CO_2) for the year 2020 in Phoenix, Arizona. *Environmental Management* 33 Supplement: S222–S228.
2003	Miller, Harvey and Elizabeth A. Wentz 2003. Geographic representation in geographic information systems and spatial analysis. *Annals of the Association of American Geographers* 93(3): 574–594.
	Wentz, Elizabeth A., Aimee F. Campbell, and Robert Houston 2003. Implementing and testing two methods of spatio-temporal data interpolation applied to tracking the movement of monkeys. *International Journal of Geographical Information Science* 17(7): 623–645.
2002	Day, Thomas A., Patricia Gober, Fusheng S. Xiong, and Elizabeth A. Wentz 2002. Temporal patterns in near-surface CO2 concentrations over contrasting vegetation types in the Phoenix metropolitan area. *Agricultural and Forest Meteorology* 110(3): 229-245.
	Wentz, Elizabeth A., Patricia Gober, Robert C. Balling, Jr., and Thomas Day 2002. Spatial patterns and determinants of carbon dioxide in an urban environment *The Annals of the Association of American Geographers* 92(1): 15–28.

Figure 3.2 illustrates the current format of my CV. The publication year appears along the left-hand side of the document and is included in the citation to the article. My name is no longer highlighted.

While the style difference here may not be relevant when you begin your career, the dates become increasingly important as your career matures. In both examples, I have maintained consistent reference style, including underlining student coauthors and italicizing journal titles. In the former, I also highlighted my name in bold so it was visible in the list and included spaces between each entry. Remember, consistency.

Consistency is important because it reflects upon your scholarly skills. If the CV is inconsistent and sloppy, it is a logical extension to assume the research is also inconsistent and sloppy. This is not the message you want to present to prospective employers or granting agencies. Proofread your CV for consistency and ask someone else to read it too.

🕐 To Do List

Develop your current CV. Do this by deciding on content and style. Be complete and detailed. Here are some steps to motivate this activity:

1. Start writing your current CV by remembering how you arrived here and not somewhere else. What else did you dream of becoming? When you were a kid, did you dream about being a professional football player? Maybe you always dreamed about becoming a photo journalist traveling to exotic places. List those five fantasy careers here:

   _____

   _____

   _____

   _____

   _____

2. What elements of your fantasy careers are part of your current path in graduate school? Do you use re-photography to analyze urban change? Maybe some of your fantasy careers are embedded in your hobbies or other interests. Consider watching the video or reading the book *The Last Lecture* by Randy Pausch to envision how your dreams can become reality.

3. Begin to write down your accomplishments; include those elements that tie into your dreams. Fill in the easy and obvious headings: contact information, education, employment, publications, presentations, and awards.

- Contact information. Make sure you have a professional e-mail address. If your e-mail is something like dorkeydot@yahoo.com, get an alias or another e-mail address. The best solution may be to use your university e-mail or Gmail instead of a personal-use address.
- For education, list post–high school degrees only. This includes certificates and degree(s) in progress.
- Like education, list any work experience you have held since high school. Include only work that contributes to your profession and not just what supported you financially. This list is not limited to just for-pay work but unpaid internships and research projects.
- If you have anything published, even publications in a newsletter, list it here. Most first-year graduate students do not have publications. By the time you finish your degree, you should aim to have several publications.

4. The following topics are typically listed next:

- Provide the names of grants—funded research proposals—in which your name is included in the proposal. If you are hired to work on a grant and your name is not included, do not list it. Most first-year students do not yet have this type of recognition, but some may—such as a fellowship to attend graduate school. Do not feel discouraged if you do not.
- List presentations next. While not always referred, they are important, because they indicate the breadth of your professional exposure. In early versions of your CV, include school-related activities such as undergraduate Capstone presentations.
- Include any awards you have received, typically post–high school. If you received an award or scholarship in high school to attend college, you should include it.
- If you have taught university courses with full responsibility, you should include them. You can also include guest lectures here if you have been asked to prepare one for an instructor.
- Unlike advice you may receive for a résumé, do not include a section called "References," and do not say, "References available upon request." This is inappropriate for a CV.

(Continued)

(Continued)

- If you are a member of professional organizations, list them last. If you are not a member, consider joining now. There are many benefits to becoming a member—particularly a student member—such as scholarships, travel awards, and job announcements.
- Include professional service activities. Some may be local, such as the graduate representative to the faculty. Others may be national, such as a graduate representative to a professional specialty group.

5. Proofread your CV more than once. Exchange your CV with fellow graduate students and be critical of one another. Overall, look for consistency and clarity.

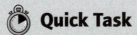 **Quick Task**

Get feedback. Ask your advisor, other faculty, and fellow graduate students to read and comment on your CV. Revise.

Feeling Stuck?

Some activities that might stimulate thoughts on your accomplishments:

1. Look at photo albums from your undergraduate education. You might see pictures of the dorm where you lived and remember you were a resident assistant your sophomore year.

2. Go to the Internet and look at the CVs of professors in your department or field. Pay particular attention to the headings they use and the early accomplishments they include. Think about things you have done in these areas.

3. Ask your advisor for several copies of his or her CV from different career stages. A current copy will show you where he or she is now. But also ask for a copy of the CV when he or she finished the PhD. Between the two documents, the trajectory of work should be evident.

4. There are numerous examples on the Internet describing how to write a CV. Keep in mind though that topic headings, order, and length can be discipline specific.

5. Ask for the CVs from other graduate students you know. Compare yourself to your peers (particularly ones ready to graduate). Do they have referred publications? How have they listed teaching and research assistantships?

Remember that the CV remains yours throughout your career and continues to change. You need to update it regularly. When you complete something CV worthy, add it immediately. If you have a paper accepted for publication, add it. If you are an invited colloquium speaker, add it. If you are asked to review a manuscript for possible publication in a referred journal, add that journal name to a list of journals where you have served as reviewer. Do not wait until you have a grant application due (which requires that you submit an updated CV) to try to sort out and list your accomplishments over the last 2 years. You will certainly forget something.

Side note: When naming the file(s) on your computer for your CV, select a naming scheme that will allow you to have multiple iterations for life. For example, you could use cv_March2013.docx.

 Action Item

Using the best version of your CV, mark (e.g., highlight, circle) past activities that form the beginning of your research trajectory. What activities have led you to where you are now and where you want to be?

Reminders

- The CV is a record of your academic path.
- The CV illustrates a research trajectory.
- Content *and* style influence how your CV is perceived.
- Consistency.
- Get feedback.
- Keep the CV up to date.

4

Area of Specialization

Introduction

The CV you just wrote is a backward-looking document that serves to record your professional accomplishments and define your research trajectory. The area-of-specialization statement (AOS) is the first forward-looking document in the development of a research proposal. It describes broadly the subject area for your research. The AOS describes your specialty within your discipline, showing the reader how you envision your research. The AOS is a short document where you state the area, define it, and explain the typical questions researchers address. In particular, it establishes these themes *from your point of view*. Since you do discuss other people's research, a few citations are required.

Some people use the AOS as a jumping-off point or an opportunity to explore a specialty area. For others, it may be the first opportunity to write formally about an interested subject area. Most students find, however, that the content in the AOS becomes integrated into the introduction of the proposal.

Function of the AOS

While the content of the AOS may become integrated into the proposal, the document described here is a stand-alone piece. The purpose of this stand-alone document is to articulate broadly the scope of the proposed research. The document serves other purposes as well. For example, it can be shared with prospective committee members to illustrate your research interests and points of view. It is convenient because it is short but effective because it provides your line of thinking. It also demonstrates your ability to express your ideas in writing. Like the CV, the AOS becomes a dynamic document that you maintain and revise over time to serve other purposes. Variations of it become the basis for research grants, cover letters for job applications, and statements for promotions.

Pieces of the AOS

The AOS document defines the top layer of a three-dimensional spiral (see Figure 4.1). The levels of the spiral represent the breadth of the material covered. The spiral analogy continues to be used in this book to illustrate how research documents, such as a proposal, "drill down" into a subject matter (the point of the spiral). But what is at the top of the spiral? What is the subject matter you are drilling into? The top of the spiral defines that broad area and describes the subfields within it or even other disciplines that connect to it. It represents the material you draw from and will eventually contribute to in your research.

Figure 4.1 The research spiral that drills into a specific research topic. The AOS represents the top slice, indicating the breadth of research you examine.

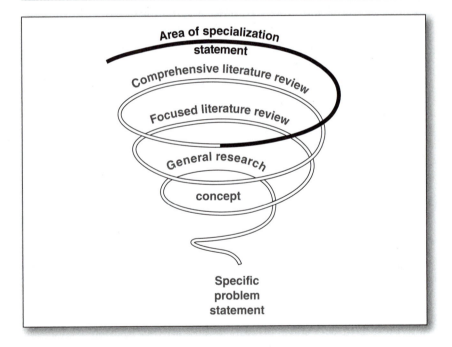

The pieces of the AOS at the top of the spiral include the subjects or subfields that encompass your work, definitions for those subjects, and a description of the problems addressed or current solutions. Many investigators (students too) include more than one subject or subfield. In an era of transdisciplinary research, these subjects can reach into multiple disciplines as well.

Some examples of subdisciplines from the social sciences include the following:

Human ecology

Demography

Linguistic anthropology

Econometrics

To Do List

State and define your subject areas. The content of this activity becomes the first paragraph of the AOS document.

1. Start by listing your discipline: _____ (e.g., anthropology, sociology, geography, economics, biology).

2. Within the discipline, list a subfield: _____. You may have more than one area you draw from (or another discipline if you're engaged in transdisciplinary research), but there should be a primary area where your work will be situated. If you draw from multiple subfields, list your secondary field(s) next: _____, _____, and _____.

3. Write a one-sentence definition for each subfield.

4. Within your subfield(s), many subjects or themes are focus areas. For example, your discipline may be sociology and within sociology, you study demography. Within demography are focus areas of research such as infant mortality, second-generation immigrant education, a specific geographic area, urban demography, and rural demography.

   For your subfield(s), list at least 10 focus areas. At this point, list as many focus areas as possible and do not worry if these are your focus area or not.

5. At least one (and possibly more than one) of the listed themes is the area where you envision your work. Circle at least one of these themes but no more than three that you consider your specialty. If you see yourself working in more than three of these themes, either you have not narrowed your interests in your discipline enough or you do not have broad enough themes identified. Fix this before you proceed.

6. Write a one-sentence definition for the themes you circled. The definition can come from the literature (use a citation), or if it is more generally known, there is no need for a specific reference. Regardless, use your own words instead of quoting so that it is apparent that the perspective is yours.

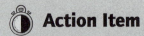

Action Item

The material from the earlier activities forms the first paragraph of the AOS. The content states your areas and defines them—from your point of view. The remaining paragraphs of the AOS provide more detail about these areas.

For each theme you circled earlier, prepare the following:

1. Identify at least one of the key players in this subject. What has their contribution been?

2. Knowledge base. What is generally known and not known about this theme?

3. Rationale. What makes this an important theme to research?

As always, define or avoid discipline-specific jargon, and do not assume your reader is an expert in the subject. Even an expert in the field (such as your advisor perhaps) can gain insight into your vision of your specific interests.

Organization of the AOS

Using the information you just assembled, you can now write your AOS. As already stated, the first paragraph names the subfield in your discipline that is a broad research domain of interest. Incorporate the definition you wrote followed by the themes you circled earlier, the themes within that subfield where you intend to do research. There are cases where there may be more than one interest, and you can include both in this first paragraph, but think clearly about which area your *research* interest is in and whether another might serve simply as a tool. For example, if you plan to use regression analysis to study educational outcomes, your area of specialization is education not statistics.

The remaining two, three, or four paragraphs describe the major issues in your specialty field that are less understood or problems needing to be solved. There is also some indication why they are important areas to address. These are not the research questions you plan to ask but more generally what is being studied. Be sure to identify key players (include references) and what they have accomplished. This is the substance of the AOS document because it identifies your perspective on unknown knowledge areas.

The last paragraph of your AOS describes the qualifications you have (or will have) to work in this area. You can provide specific information on previous degrees, coursework (that you have taken or plan to take), or other experiences you have. This is the link back to your CV and provides the tie to the trajectory of your work.

Some Constraints

- Most AOSs are 1,200–1,500 words with two to three references. The format is your choice (e.g., font, spacing). The goal is to make the style legible.
- The AOS is about the subject area of your research. It *does not* describe your research problem or specific goals—save that for the research statement (Chapter 10). It does, however, need to be more specific than just a list of broad research areas.
- Do not undermine the importance of this short document or underestimate how long it will take to write. Ask your advisor and other graduate students to read it and provide feedback. Revise it multiple times to make it read well and say exactly what you intend to say.

The Language of Research

For some students, writing the AOS may seem pedantic. In fact, some professors may believe students should already have a firm grasp of their field and specialization. In such cases, these activities may or may not offer tools to jump-start or motivate your research. Nevertheless, it is a writing exercise that provides you with the opportunity to describe your research area using the "language of research." Craft what *you* say well by describing what *they* said in the appropriate language. Use this exercise as an opportunity to demonstrate your ability to communicate in the language of research. Formal writing does not need to be difficult but does need to be precise. More specifics on writing style are covered in Chapter 6.

Reminders

- The AOS defines and describes your specialization.
- Define jargon.
- Get feedback and revise.
- The document is forward looking.
- The AOS does not describe your research.

5

Effective Reading

Introduction

Chapter 3 covers the CV, which describes your past academic accomplishments. In the world of proposal writing, the CV serves to guide and build your research trajectory and to demonstrate you have the skills necessary to complete the proposed activities. Chapter 4 frames the knowledge area for your research. This chapter develops skills you need to move forward toward creating your own knowledge.

Creating new knowledge begins by comprehending existing knowledge. You have an article you need or want to read. You have read the title, the abstract, and a bit more. These pieces have told you this paper could be important to your research. What's next? Grab a coffee, hit the comfy chair, and read. Except for the coffee, this is a recipe for nodding off. There is nothing like a journal article to cure insomnia. Your eyes pass over a paragraph and little is comprehended. It is not effective. And because you will likely need to read it again, you are also inefficient. This chapter describes how to read both effectively and efficiently to maximize your efforts in comprehending the literature.

Reasons to Read

The main reasons to read seem pretty obvious, but perhaps there are some less obvious reasons to introduce here. The obvious reasons for reading are to understand the present state of knowledge on a particular topic, to be aware of the methods used, and to be clear on the gaps in that knowledge base. These reasons describe the knowledge needed to write a literature review (discussed in depth in Chapter 7). There are more subtle reasons to read too: to use excellent published articles as writing templates (see Chapter 6), to learn the people in the field, to know when and maybe how certain ideas developed, and to be broadly aware of the research community. These more subtle reasons are discussed here.

The first of the less-obvious reasons to read is to use excellent articles as writing templates for your own future articles. These templates can be used for their stylistic, organizational, or methodological approach. The article may not even be directly related to your own work but can still provide guidance on how to organize, structure, or plan research. For example, a paper may provide ideas on how to describe methods or a data collection approach.

A second reason to read is to learn who is doing the work in your field. Knowing "who" is important because you may want to write to them for additional information about their research, meet them at a professional conference, or invite them to your department for invited colloquia. Established researchers have avenues of research into particular themes. When you meet people at conferences or go to job interviews, it is helpful if you know the people and their avenues of research.

Related to knowing who's who in your field is the expression that goes something like "it isn't about *what* you know, it is about *who* you know." While I like to believe that merit (and by association *what* you know) still matters, there is something true about the expression that *who* you know is also important. The academic world remains small, and contacts can provide leads into the job market.

After knowing who is doing the work, learning when the work was done becomes important. Disciplines undergo transitions in thought, theories, and methods. Although considered controversial, Kuhn (1962) described these transitions as paradigm shifts. Understanding the chronology of your field and how individuals participated in that chronology (were they at the leading edge of an emerging paradigm or were they central to the development) gives you a broader understanding of how ideas develop.

A final reason to read is to be aware of and know something about the research outside your own field—for at least three reasons. First, there is no doubt you will focus the majority of your time and efforts on literature related to your specific subfield. But you also need to know how your work fits into a broader research framework. Without reading pieces in this broader framework, it is difficult to know this. Second, interdisciplinary work is becoming a common operating mode. If you have read outside your own subject area, you will be better equipped to understand research perspectives from disciplinary and interdisciplinary collaborators. Third, you will likely engage as a professional (whether as a professor or a researcher) with students and colleagues who seek advice on myriad topics.

The obvious reason to read is to learn and understand the existing body of knowledge in your own field; this reason extends to the broader knowledge base. What contributes to understanding the world? Is the view accurate? Are the views of others the same as yours? You must know what other people have done to demonstrate that the knowledge you contribute is new.

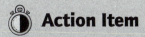

Action Item

Identify a person (or two) from your subject area who you would like to meet. E-mail the person a substantive question about his or her work, mentioning too that you are researching a similar subject. Consider working with the colloquium coordinator to invite him or her to visit your institution. Help coordinate the visit.

What to Read

There is a lot of literature out there—good, bad, relevant, and irrelevant. Your job is to sort through this and synthesize it into something meaningful. Asimov (1958) reports on this challenge in the essay "The Sound of Panting." The title itself identifies the often-overwhelming feeling associated with keeping in touch with the literature. Your time is precious and to find the right book or article to read can be challenging. It is easy to spend a considerable amount of time on an article that in the end may be unrelated to your research. The goal here is to learn how to be selective and efficient with reading.

PEER REVIEWED OR NOT

In the academic world, the literature is generally divided into two categories: peer reviewed and non–peer reviewed. *Peer reviewed* means the document (prior to publication) was evaluated by experts, and those experts advised the editor that the manuscript contributed to the body of knowledge. Non–peer reviewed works are publications that have not undergone this process. In general, peer-reviewed work is considered more reliable, more correct, and just generally "better." However, it probably is not surprising that there are plenty of excellent and substantive contributions to the literature in non–peer reviewed outlets. Likewise, there is plenty of "poor" material in peer-reviewed outlets. The only real difference between them therefore is that experts in the field have sanctioned a peer-review article.

In the social sciences, peer-reviewed outlets are typically journals. In some cases books and conference proceedings are also peer reviewed. Journals, however, tend to have a more rigorous review process than books or proceedings. Journals listed in the *Journal Citation Reports*, published by Thomas Reuters, are all peer reviewed. The contents of these journals are accessible via the Web of Science, a searchable online database (described in detail shortly). Some peer-reviewed journals do not appear in the *Journal Citation Reports* because they do not meet the citation requirements either due to few citations or because the journal is relatively new.

It is less clear when books are peer reviewed. In some cases, the editor or publisher indicates that at the front of the book. Reliability of the editor or publisher can provide insight into the review process and the potential quality of the contribution. There are two types of academic books. One is led by an editor(s) and contains chapters written by different authors. In this case, the editor(s) is responsible for obtaining publishable manuscripts from separate authors, reviewing the contributions (or sending them out for peer review), and organizing the content in a meaningful way. The advantage of this type of book is that it provides a comprehensive examination of a topic in a single source. The other type is an author-led book, which is written entirely by a single or small group of authors. Typically there is tighter cohesion between chapters because the author(s) has written all of the pieces. In some cases (depending on the publisher), the book is also peer reviewed. The advantage of this type of book is the unity and in-depth perspective on a single topic.

Like books, conference proceedings may or may not be peer reviewed. Again, the preface of the proceedings (or a website) may or may not provide information on the publication process. Ideally, it's something you know, especially if the conference is associated with your primary discipline. Conference proceedings are a compilation of the presented papers or posters at a conference. They are distributed as books or compact disks at the conference or following it. In some fields, the peer-review process occurs prior to the conference (through a referred abstract) and then again when the paper is submitted. In other cases, abstracts and conference papers are simply submitted and published without any peer review. The advantage of conference papers is they are typically short, providing specific insight into a problem. Furthermore, because the review process tends to be shorter than journals (less than a year compared to 18 months or more), the contributions tend to be the most recent effort by the author.

There are other outlets known to be non–peer reviewed. These include white papers and project websites. These are valuable sources of information, particularly for up-to-date information on a research topic. A white paper is a manuscript written with a specific objective that may have to do with reporting on a particular position or viewpoint, explaining the details of a particular methodology, solving a specific problem, or introducing a new idea. It is not a scientific, published paper because of the directed nature of the work. Scientific workshops often require participants to prepare and submit a white paper prior to the workshop to initiate workshop discussions.

The second common form of non–peer reviewed outlets is websites. Within this vast amount of information, the most common scientific resource is project, research lab, or investigator websites. These scientifically based websites provide public information on the research goals and outcomes of a project. Typically there are descriptions of research goals, the associated people, publications (peer reviewed and non–peer reviewed), presentations, and downloadable products (e.g., software or data). Project websites allow you to see who is involved in a project as well as download useful material.

MEASURES OF SUCCESS FOR PEER-REVIEWED MATERIAL

Given the vast amount of material accessible, it is difficult to know what is good and what is not. The closest index to describe "good" is a journal's impact factor. Yearly, referred journals in the social sciences (those listed in the *Journal Citation Reports*) are assigned an impact factor (IF). The IF is a number that represents the "importance" of a journal in a particular field based on the number of citations of the articles published in the journal. Generally, higher numbers mean a journal has more papers cited, lower IF numbers mean fewer—although the algorithm is not this straightforward.

Some scholars use the IF as representative of the quality of a journal and subsequently the articles that appear in it. In this case, a higher IF means higher-quality papers. In some sense, this is true because "better" papers are cited more often than "bad" papers. This idea, however, is misleading because papers are cited for a variety of reasons and not necessarily because they are "good." Literature review articles for example often receive many citations because they summarize the literature, thereby freeing the citing author from performing this task. Figure 5.1 illustrates the increasing IF factor over time for the journal the *American Anthropologist*. The positive trend may suggest the journal's "quality" is improving.

Finding Material to Read

In a typical university course, the instructor assigns most of the class readings. In graduate courses, it is often up to the student to find the right material to read. There are several ways to approach this, the best being to use all the resources available. There are tools to assist you with finding the right pieces for your work.

CITATION INDICES

Most universities provide digital access to a variety of citation indices. These are searchable databases of books, magazines, newspapers, journals,

Figure 5.1   Graph showing the trend of the *American Anthropologist* impact factor (IF) over time.

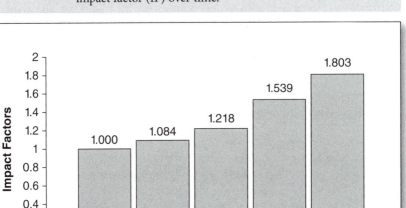

Source: Graphic obtained from ISI Web of Knowledge *Journal Citation Reports* website, April 2012.

conference proceedings, and other published material. The names of common searchable resources are listed in Table 5.1. The material is searchable based on several fields, including keywords, source title, author name, year published, peer reviewed (for indices that have non–peer reviewed contents), language, and document type. For many of them, a subscription is required. Fortunately, universities subscribe to many of them and you can access them either through campus computers (which tend to provide direct access) or by logging in through your university computer account. The search returns a list of documents that meet the search criteria. In some cases, there is also a direct link to the actual document. An item from the list at minimum provides:

author name(s),

year published,

source,

title, and

abstract.

Sometimes included are:

links to the full source, depending on the availability (free or subscription),

the number of times it has been cited plus a list (or links when possible) of papers that cited it,

the papers cited, and

related articles.

The list is also sortable by fields that could include:

year published,

document type, or

highest to lowest or lowest to highest number of citations.

Table 5.1   List of common searchable resources available either by subscription or free.

Index Name	Description	Document Types*
ABI/Inform	Business research database	Journal articles, news sources
Academic Search Premier, EBSCO Publishing	Multidiscipline database	Journals, magazines, and other sources
CINAHL, EBSCO Publishing	Nursing and allied health database	Journals, magazines, and other sources
Dissertations and theses	PhD and MA/MS from multiple disciplines	Dissertations and MA/MS theses
eBooks (NetLibrary)	Multiple disciplines	Digital books
Economist Intelligence Unit (EIU)	Resources from *The Economist*	Reports, articles, webinars, and podcasts
ERIC	Education	Journals
Google Scholar	Multiple disciplines	Journals, proceedings, magazines, with the option to select patents, legal opinions
IEEE Xplore	Engineering and technology	Searchable for IEEE publications, journals, and conferences

(Continued)

Table 5.1   (Continued)

Index Name	Description	Document Types*
JSTOR	Peer reviewed from the liberal arts and sciences	Searchable for the journals JSTOR content
LexisNexis Academic	Business, government, and legal	Journal articles, reports, legal documents
MDConsult	Medical	Books, journals, review articles
Medline (Ovid)	Biomedical, health	Journal articles
Naxos Music Library	Music	Recordings
PsycInfo	Psychology	Peer reviewed, books, dissertations
PubMed	Biomedical and life sciences	Journals, books, online books
Web of Science	Multiple disciplines	Peer-reviewed journals
Worldcat (OCLC FirstSearch)	Multiple disciplines	Journals, magazines, books, electronic resources

After you decide which index to use, the next step is to build and use a list of keywords relevant to your subject. Keywords can be tricky to develop—it is often a process of trial and error to determine the combination that reveals the literature you want to find. Too-general keyword combinations return too many references. For example, "data" and "accuracy" returned 118,000 references in the Web of Science (accessed February 22, 2013). Similarly, too-specific keyword combinations return too few or even no references. It is likely keyword combinations will return references to the literature you expect to find as well as unrelated references simply because of the keywords you selected.

⏱ To Do List

1. Write a list of keywords, including alternative spellings and forms (e.g., *theory, theoretical*). Select keywords from the articles you have read so far as a starting point.

2. Use a combination of one or two keywords to get a first search. Be systematic about this, recording which combinations you used and how many hits (number of records in the list) you got.

Depending on the database, a good first search is around 200 or so hits. With this size list, review whether the keywords returned the type of articles you expected. Sometimes searches return 4,000 or 1,000,000 hits (too many to review) and sometimes only one or two hits (not enough).

3. After you establish a reasonable list, use sorting tools to examine publications from the oldest to newest and highest to lowest cited. This overview gives the big picture of your list and helps you narrow the search.

4. Narrow the search to about 50 hits. This means adding new keywords to the search, specifying certain databases or document types, limiting yourself to specific journals, and restricting the publication year or where keywords occur in the record.

The search engine of the citation index software uses Boolean operators and keywords to select material. Boolean operators are functions in mathematical set theory, where a set is a collection of objects. In this case, our set is a database containing books, articles, and material. For simplicity in the following examples, I refer to the contents of the database as articles (assuming referred journal articles), but the type of material in the database depends completely on the resource. The operators place criteria on the selection to pick the right combination of objects from the set. The main operators used in the case of citation indices are AND, OR, and NOT.

AND returns the intersection between two or more sets. With two keywords in the topic search box (e.g., *migration, health*) all records with both words in the title, keyword list, or abstract are included in the returned list.

OR represents the union between two sets. With two keywords in the topic search box (e.g., *migration, health*), all records with either word in the title, keyword list, or abstract are included in the return list

NOT removes items from the set containing the keyword. NOT is typically used with the AND and OR operators simultaneously to narrow search results. It makes the set either the same size or smaller than the previous set because hits are removed.

For example, consider this search in the Web of Science (April 2012):

Topic: migration AND health

Return: 4,713 records. A sample record highlighting the words *health* (in the title and the abstract) and *migration* (in the abstract alone) are shown in Figure 5.2.

Figure 5.2 This is a sample record from Web of Science showing migration and health in the record.

Factors affecting children's oral health : perceptions among Latino parents

Author(s): Cortes, DE (Cortes, Dharma E.)1; Reategui-Sharpe, L (Reategui-Sharpe, Ludmila)2; Spiro, A (Spiro, Avron, III)2·3; Garcia, RI (Garcia, Raul I.)2

Source: JOURNAL OF PUBLIC HEALTH DENTISTRY **Volume:** 72 **Issue:** 1 **Pages:** 82–89 **DOI:** 10.1111/j.1752-7325.2011.00287.x **Published:** WIN 2012

Times Cited: 0 (from Web of Science)

Cited References: 20 [view related records] ▦Citation Map

Abstract: Objective: The objective of this study is to understand factors that influence the oral health-related behaviors of Latino children, as reported by their parents.

Methods: Focus groups and in-depth interviews assessed parental perceptions, experiences, attributions, and beliefs regarding their children's oral health. Guiding questions focused on a) the participant's child dental experiences; b) the impact of dental problems on the child's daily activities, emotions, self-esteem; c) parental experiences coping with child's dental problems; and d) hygienic and dietary habits. Participants were purposively sampled from dental clinics and public schools with a high concentration of Latinos; 92 urban low-income Latino Spanish-speaking parents participated. Transcriptions of the audio files were thematically analyzed using a grounded theory approach.

Results: Parents's explanations of their children's dental experiences were categorized under the following themes: caries and diet, access to dental care, migration experiences, and routines.

Conclusions: Findings revealed fundamental multilevel (i.e., individual/ child, family, and community) factors that are important to consider for future interventions to reduce oral health disparities: behaviors leading to caries, parental knowledge about optimal oral health, access to sugary foods within the living environment and to fluoridated water as well as barriers to oral health care such as lack of health insurance or limited health insurance coverage, among others.

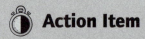

Action Item

Craft a keyword list of 10 to 20 keywords from your area of specialization. Using the steps listed earlier, create a reference list containing 50 or so articles related to your field or topic of interest.

Figure 5.3 shows a record was not in the first search because it contains only the word *migration* (in the title) and not the word *health*.

Figure 5.3   This record shows only migration because the Boolean 'or' was used.

Does Labour migration Offer Opportunities for Meeting Prospective Spouses? The Case of Migrant Workers in Cambodia

Author(s): Yagura, K (Yagura, Kenjiro)

Source: POPULATION SPACE AND PLACE **Volume:** 18 **Issue:** 3 **Pages:** 277–294 **DOI:** 10.1002/psp.683 **Published:** MAY–JUN 2012

Times Cited: 0 (from Web of Science)

Cited References: 18 [view related records] 📧**Citation Map**

Abstract: In the rural areas of developing countries, the children of poor families are at a disadvantaged position in the local marriage market. Labour migration may offer opportunities to find a suitable spouse because an acquaintance in the migration destination may emerge as a prospective spouse. This paper examines whether or not this happens in reality. Econometric analysis of the data of unmarried migrant workers in Phnom Penh indicated that those who do not expect their parents to give them land prefer marrying someone they meet in Phnom Penh rather than someone from their own place of origin. This suggests that those who encounter difficulties in finding a partner in their place of origins actively seek a spouse at the migration destination. The findings indicate that labour migration introduces changes in the formation of families, which consequently influences familial relationships. Copyright (c) 2011 John Wiley & Sons, Ltd.

Other combinations of keywords *migration* and *health* with different Boolean operators return different records.

Topic: migration OR health
    Return: 1,126,079 hits

Topic: migration AND health NOT children
    Return: 4,117 hits

Topic: migration OR health NOT children
    Return: 1,021,557 hits

REFERENCE LISTS

Dissertations, proposals, and published papers all have citations. These lists of references become an additional source of material to evaluate. As you read (see Active Reading section that follows), identify articles in then bibliography you want to acquire. One approach is to highlight them as you read the article and then go back through just the bibliography in case you missed something. Ideally, you should immediately add the references to your database or, better yet, just obtain the articles. Waiting to do either never works because the article is put aside and replaced by the next one on the list.

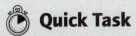

Quick Task

Select an article you have read. Identify and obtain related articles from the list of references.

JOURNALS

After you have read a few articles, you will have a general sense of "good" journals. The impact factor is one determinant of a good journal, but you will also learn which journals publish papers on your topic. To explore further what these particular journals publish, go to their websites or visit the collection in the library and search previous issues for related papers. You may even find a special issue containing a group of articles related to your topic. In addition to the searchable citation indices described earlier, journal websites also provide searchable access to previous issues. If your library has a subscription to the journal, then you also have direct access to the articles.

There are advantages and disadvantages to focusing on journals in selected disciplines. The advantages of focusing on a particular journal or journals are they may serve as a future outlet for your own work, represent a particular discourse where you are engaged, and allow you to develop depth of knowledge. The disadvantage is that this focus may limit your scope of understanding or analyzing a problem. In addition to journals in your own field, open up your search parameters to explore the manner in which other disciplines evaluate and understand your topic. Search engines, such as those described earlier, allow you to easily open up access to journals in all fields, not just your own.

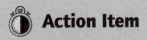

Action Item

Select a journal that appears more than once in your bibliography. Identify its IF. Search for more articles from that journal using the journal's searching tools. Add these articles to your bibliography.

PROFESSORS

Without a doubt, professors will have ideas on what (and who) to read related to your topic. However, some professors recoil when a student sends an e-mail saying, "I'm researching topic X, can you please send me some references related to this topic?" It sends a message that the student does not want to do his or her own work (the necessary searches). Instead, the preferred approach is when a student sends an e-mail with a bibliography (around 10 articles) of papers on the topic they are interested in studying. The student can then ask, "Here is where I have started. What other authors, journals, or keywords do you [the professor] suggest I use for my searches?" Professors may reply with a reference or so and, sometimes, a PDF or two of articles they have on hand. Furthermore, it opens the channel for future dialog between the student and professor that a particular subject interests that student. The professor may send articles of potential interest in the future.

Action Item

Take the list of articles and keywords to your advisor (or another member of the faculty) and indicate this as your starting point. Ask if they have any suggestions for other authors, journals, or keywords to help expand your search.

GENERAL WEB SEARCHES

General web searches are a bit hit and miss when it comes to high-quality references. The advantage of a general web search is that instead of finding a particular book or article on a subject, you might find instead an overview of their research. On a website like this, papers and other published material are usually available. Another advantage of a web search is that non–peer reviewed papers are more likely to appear. While they have not undergone the rigor of the peer-review process, they may be more up to date.

The downside of web searches, as anyone knows, is that they can be faulty and unpredictable and reveal material unrelated to your query. Any papers or information found needs to be viewed critically. A web search will be only as good as the web-crawling algorithm and the way the webpages themselves are constructed. Unlike a searchable index (where everything with a particular keyword is found), a web search may not find everything on a subject—just the most popular.

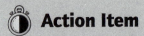

Action Item

Learn about the people in your field. From the final list you created earlier select at least three investigators with two articles each (they don't have to be exclusively first author). Learn more about who these three investigators are. Investigate where they are employed, their primary discipline, the major themes they study.

How to Read

One overarching reason to read is self-education on methods, people, or a particular subject. As educators know, there are different learning styles. Likewise, there are different reading styles for academic learning: passive and active. Passive reading is what most people consider reading: sitting with a document, passing your eyes over consecutive words, and comprehending the message intended by the author(s). Active reading involves deeper engagement with the text by the reader—taking notes and reading for a specific purpose. Effective and efficient reading requires the use of both passive and active reading.

PASSIVE READING

Passive reading is engaging with a document without any visible external action. Passive reading does *not* suggest the reader is not absorbing what he or she is reading. Instead it implies that the reader is just reading. Much like passive learning, passive reading aims to inform the reader with the knowledge contained within the document. The article will have some imprint on memory, but it is difficult to retain details or extensive content.

Passive reading is often used as a first pass through an article to identify whether it should be flagged as high, medium, or low importance. Reading an article passively involves reading the abstract first, then reading the conclusions, and then reading in detail the methods. From this approach, the reader should be able to know what the article is about, its key contribution, and how the research was conducted. This type of reading is both effective and efficient because it focuses on a specific outcome: Does this article warrant further attention?

Passive reading is often associated with generalized *skimming*, and I want to emphasize that this is not the case. Skimming an article is both ineffective and inefficient. Skimming implies that you read bits, skip over bits, and try to figure out what the article is about without actually reading it. Passive reading instead is a more systematic approach. It is effective because the reader targets specific sections, and it is efficient because other sections are saved for later, more active, reading.

ACTIVE READING

Active reading implies the reader is participating more deliberately in the reading effort. This does not necessarily mean concentrating more or even taking more time to read but instead reading with a specific purpose. That purpose may be simple and not take very long, or it may mean longer engagement with a particular document. In order of estimated time to completion (shortest to longest), the following are active-reading tasks:

- Finding the key take-home message: Each book, article, or white paper is written with a specific message. That message represents the core idea a particular document contributes to the body of knowledge. For shorter documents (e.g., journal articles), the new knowledge is specific and fills a small hole in knowledge. For longer documents (e.g., a book), the new knowledge is a broader conceptual idea that fills a moderate or large hole in knowledge.
- Extracting key methods (e.g., data sources, study location, and general methods)
- Taking notes
- Writing a critical précis of the article. A critical précis is an article summary that includes the main ideas of the article plus an evaluation of the work as a contribution to the field. Typical length is from 800 to 1,500 words.

Each time you read, decide if you are going to use passive- or active-reading skills. There is a time and a place for both types.

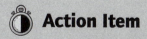

Action Item

Using the bibliography earlier, use passive-reading skills to flag the articles on the list as high, medium, or low relevance to your topic.

With one article of your choice (make it a good one), use active-reading skills to write a detailed critical précis to share with your advisor.

Organizing What You Read

There are two overarching ways to keep track of what you have read. The first is to approach it systematically. The second is a bit more ad hoc.

SYSTEMATIC

There are commercial and freeware products such as RefWorks or EndNote to record, store, and search a personal archive of literature. You can incorporate your own notes along with written summaries into the database. Several software products such as Zotero organize and provide access to article references, personal notes, and downloaded manuscripts.

> Advantages: The software generates a formatted bibliography in the style appropriate to the outlet (this is a big deal), you go to one place on your computer to find your articles, and you can search your own database for items you have read (or meant to read).

> Disadvantages: It demands time to maintain (and you need to be meticulous with this), software needs to be learned, and the software may need to be purchased.

AD HOC

The ad-hoc approach means you use non–reference based software (e.g., spreadsheet or word processing) or handwritten notes to keep your material organized. More often than not, the material is organized by project, so the literature is stored with the data, analysis, and written papers. The advantages and disadvantages for approaching article organization are essentially the inverse to the systematic approach:

> Advantages: It requires less time and organization is performed on a case-by-case basis.

> Disadvantages: Stylistic bibliography formatting is performed case by case*, previous articles you have collected are in a searchable system, depends on your memory of when you read an article and what project it was associated with.

You can still use reference software to generate formatted bibliographies on a case-by-case basis, but the tool becomes less effective as a researching device for future papers.

Read Daily

Previous chapters discussed how graduate students are expected to create new knowledge. This new knowledge does not emerge from thin air but rather by "standing on the shoulders of giants." Reading regularly (plus comprehending, synthesizing, and writing) what the giants have contributed to knowledge builds the foundation on which to create new knowledge. Reading therefore comes at the beginning, middle, and end of research; in other words, throughout the process of creating new knowledge.

Incorporating reading into your daily routine is essential for success in academia. Just like writing, reading effectively and efficiently is a skill that needs to be developed and maintained by daily practice. This is because reading the literature is the starting point for all academic endeavors. It is important to know and describe what other researchers have done before you so you can identify and fill in the holes in the knowledge.

Quick Task

Devote, at minimum, 20 minutes per day to academic reading. Incorporate this reading time into your schedule at a regular time.

Action Item

Find a reading buddy or a small reading group that meets regularly (e.g., weekly) to discuss selected articles. Each week, one person selects an article and distributes it to the group. The following week, meet to discuss the article as a group with the person who selected the article leading the discussion. It is fun and interesting because you will read a variety of papers and everyone has the opportunity to hear and discuss other people's thoughts on the paper. Keep it energized by making the schedule one semester at a time.

Stop Reading

"Read Daily" followed by "Stop Reading" is certainly an ironic contradiction. It is presented here however because of times students "spin their wheels" in the literature and never move forward into creating their own knowledge. They seem to believe they do not yet know enough (fear or anxiety may contribute to this) to make a substantive contribution to the literature. Deciding when to stop searching and reading and when to start doing their own work is challenging for some students. Some key indicators that you may be spinning your wheels are:

a) when the same articles appear in new searches;

b) when the article, chapter, or book is in obscure and hard-to-find publications; and

c) when you have been at it for many months and are not yet developing your own research.

The real advice here of course is to continually read *and* write. These are not mutually exclusive events. As you read, you are writing. As you write, you are returning to the literature to read. Even when you are writing up your dissertation, the literature continues to move forward, and you need to continue to be aware of new information within and around your field.

Reminders

- Learn what was studied, who studied it, and when it was studied.
- Use a variety of search tools to find material to read.
- Organize your material in a way that you can keep track of it.
- Engage in both passive and active reading.
- Read daily.

References

Asimov, I. (1958). *Only a trillion*. London: Abelard-Schuman.

Kuhn, T. S. (1962). *The structure of scientific revolutions*. Chicago: University of Chicago Press.

6

Effective Writing

Introduction

The previous chapter discussed reading, an important tool for academic success. The corollary to effective reading is effective writing. Writing is an essential skill needed to finish your proposal, complete your dissertation, and be successful in academia generally. Because it is a skill and not simply an inherent talent, it is possible for anyone with average or above average intelligence to learn how to write. Like any skill, it takes time and demands practice. Practice means receiving feedback on writing and responding to the feedback to improve a given document.

There are two important writing elements to any document: content and presentation. The content is the essence of the scholarship, the contribution. It is the theory, observations, methods, results, and interpretation of the results relative to the existing literature. Each section of the document, each paragraph, and each sentence must have content. The presentation is the text, tables, and graphics used to communicate the content through organized structure, accurate grammar, and consistent format. The structure refers to how the overall message is organized and reported. Grammar is the correct usage of the English language. Format is how the document looks—the font, spacing, and page size. Each of these writing elements must be solid for a manuscript to effectively communicate your message.

Deciding what to write and how to rewrite requires a toolbox. The tools elaborated on later in this chapter are content, structure, grammar, and format. These tools can be used to provide feedback to others, analyze your own work, interpret feedback, and modify a manuscript. Using the toolbox burdens authors though because it requires a commitment to modify and delete sections. It can be emotionally difficult to delete entire paragraphs (or pages) that no longer fit. It is necessary though because it improves the delivery of the message.

Two caveats to this chapter: First, it is not a comprehensive guide to academic writing, especially the section on grammatical issues. Instead this chapter focuses on issues and mistakes commonly made by graduate students. I introduce simple tools to improve writing. Another caveat to this chapter is that the Action Items focus on journal article writing instead of proposal writing. I draw on journal articles because they are easier to access and, more often than not, are well written because they have undergone extensive review.

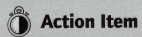

Action Item

The Action Items in this chapter use previously published works to practice using the writing toolbox. To support this, find a referred journal article in your field from a reputable journal. Notice how the introduction tells you what the paper is about; read the conclusion and notice how it tells you what was in the paper. These are key elements in an effective scientific paper.

Content

Content is the essential part of the paper—the message—the contribution made to the literature. Smooth or fancy writing does not cover up weak content. The content needs to be carefully considered at each level: the document, the paragraph, and the sentence. At every stage, you need to think about these questions:

What is the message of the sentence I just wrote?

How does it support my paragraph?

What is the main message of this paragraph?

Does the topic sentence reflect the message of the paragraph?

How do the paragraphs link together to support the section's key message?

What is the take-home message of my document?

This chapter helps you answer each of these questions.

Searching and indexing systems use the words in the title, abstract, and keywords to index individual work among the vast quantity of literature. If you want your work found, you need to stick to conventional terminology in the title, abstract, and keyword list. Nevertheless, terminology needs to be selected to distinguish your work from others with effective word choices.

The title of your document (whether a paper or proposal) must provide keywords to indicate the general topic of the work and detail words to clarify the specific contribution you intend to make. The title is an invitation to readers to continue to read. It needs to balance between being too general and too detailed.

In addition to the words in the title, keywords clarify the contribution a document makes to the literature. Some of these words may be in the title and others may not. Be sure you add keywords that are not in your title to make the keyword list meaningful. When you submit a manuscript or a proposal for review, you are often asked to select keywords. These words are used to identify your work into a larger body of research. They are used to match your work with prospective reviewers.

The abstract is a stand-alone, condensed version of the entire work. Like the title, it is an invitation to readers to continue to read. It therefore contains key ideas associated with the work but minimizes jargon and abbreviations. A colleague described the abstract to me as a "bullion cube." A bullion cube is condensed cooking stock; it contains all of the flavor and seasonings of broth but lacks the volume. Likewise, the abstract is a condensed document, completely containing the content of the document—what it is about, why it is important, what others have done, what is different about this approach, and the findings. Like the bullion cube, it contains the essence of the entire work without the volume. The abstract is not an introduction or, worse, the first paragraph of the manuscript.

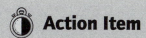

Action Item

Read the title of the manuscript you selected in the introduction. What level of balance between generality or specificity does it provide? How do the keywords enhance your understanding of what this paper contributes to the literature?

Read the abstract of the journal article you selected. Identify and write down the findings of the paper. What key contribution does this paper make to the scientific literature?

Note: While the proposal you write as an activity in this book will not have results or key findings, it needs to have a main point. The main point of a proposal is the expected findings, or the understanding or insight gained from the proposed activities.

Structure

The second tool in the toolbox is structure. Structure refers to the organization of the content; the order the content is presented to the reader. Structure needs to be designed and considered for the whole document—all paragraphs and each sentence. Planning and considering structure through outlining improves the presentation of the content.

DOCUMENT

Document structure is the framework for the entire piece. Readers need to know what to expect as they are reading. Therefore, document structure goes something like this:

> *Tell them what you are going to tell them.* The reader needs to know this to follow the story. Plot twists and surprise endings common in novels are unacceptable in technical writing.
>
> *Tell them.* Provide the content in a systematic and predictable order.
>
> *Tell them what you told them.* Summarize and highlight the key points of the manuscript.

While the process seems to include quite a bit of unnecessary repetition, it instead provides the reader with an understanding of what to expect so the message is as clear as possible.

The best way to ensure a document is structured effectively is based on an old lesson: the outline. Outlining is a technique known to all. It bears repeating however because it seems that some people have forgotten its utility or remain averse to it. Unfortunately too, word processing software has led to an abandonment of the outline as a tool, which is not in the best interest of quality writing. The lesson is to write an outline of your document to organize your ideas into a logical structure. Use the outline too in revising your document so you do not forget the overarching structure.

An outline is an abstract representation of a written document showcasing the key elements, the order they are to be presented, and the linkages between them. The key elements are the content—the message delivered in each section. The order in which they are presented is the organization of those ideas into a logical sequence. The linkages illustrate the transition from one section to the next but also how the message refers back to previous sections.

The primary reason you outline is because, in the end, you want a document that makes sense to the reader. The outline assists writers in achieving this goal. The process of outlining helps you organize key thoughts, such as main elements that need to be stated. It helps to maintain a vision of the "forest" (i.e., the main message) when crafting the "trees" (i.e., individual sentences). Without it, you may write paragraphs and sentences and forget the overarching frame. When you outline, you create that overarching frame and fill in the details later.

Effective outlines deliver content through complete sentences. It is insufficient to have vague bullet points for sections and subsections of your outline. When an outline is incomplete, it reflects incomplete ideas on content. It also makes it difficult for someone else (such as your advisor) to read and comment on your outline. Full-sentence outlines are the most effective way to ensure the necessary details are included.

Effective outlines also identify relationships between sections. The order of the sections is not just linear from top to bottom but also internally connected. For example, Figure 6.1 illustrates a common yet generalized outline of a scientific paper. This structure is commonly used in the social and behavioral sciences but is not the only structure used. Notice how the arrows on the right flow from top to bottom. This illustrates the flow of how papers can be read and how the ideas link from section to section.

The organization also shows an internal structure, or a conversation of the content that speaks back to prior sections. The arrows on the right side of Figure 6.1 show how the topics flow from one section to the next in a linear manner. The arrows on the left side of Figure 6.1 represent how the content of one section "answers" a prior one. The paper is a dialog from beginning to end

Figure 6.1 Linkages between sections of a scientific paper. The right-hand side shows how one section transitions to the next. The left-hand side illustrates how the content of each section references topics presented in previous sections.

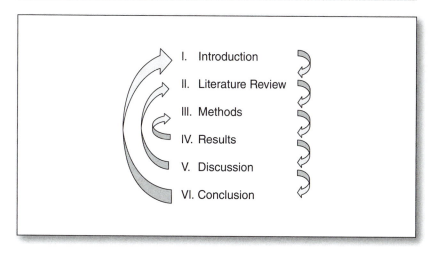

with internal (backward-focusing) linkages. The introduction tells the reader what the paper is about; the conclusion reiterates that by describing the contribution the paper made. The literature review describes prior research; the discussion describes how the paper contributes to that literature. The methods describe the approach the current research uses; the results describe the outcome of those methods. This holistic view of the document is best visualized through an outline. The outline must show both the external flow of one section to another and also the internal connections between sections.

Creswell (2009) used an hourglass analogy to describe this organization. His analogy suggests the top and bottom of the document (i.e., the introduction and conclusion) are broad and general and the middle sections (i.e., the methods and results) are narrow and detailed. This analogy is similar to the research spiral described in this book, which also suggests that content needs to transition from broad to narrow.

🕐 To Do List

Using the paper you selected earlier, re-create the outline of the manuscript. If the paper has subheadings (and most do), these can be used as outline headings.

Following this lead, the outline for the article by Glick and Hohmann-Marriott (2007) is as follows:

    I. Introduction

    II. Background
        A. Generation status and family experience in the United States
        B. Racial identification and country of origin
        C. Language proficiency
        D. Family resources

    III. The current study

    IV. Data and methods
        A. Outcome measures
        B. Independent variables
        C. Family resources and involvement

    V. Results

    VI. Discussion

    VII. References

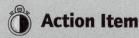

Action Item

As I did here, highlight generic headings in one color (potential template features) and those specific to the study in a different color. For the headings or subheadings specific to the topic, notice where they are in the document. In the case of Glick and Hohmann-Marriott (2007), items A–D in Section II represent the different themes of the literature review.

Convert the outline into a generic template that you can use as a possible model:

    I. Introduction

    II. Background

        A. _____
        B. _____
        C. _____ themes in the literature
        D. _____

    III. The current study

    IV. Data and methods

        A. Outcome measures
        B. Independent variables
        C. _____ data or method specific to study

    V. Results

    VI. Discussion

    VII. References

The outline you construct—whether based on a template or not—reflects a structure and order for the reader. Unlike a novel read from beginning to end, a scientific document *may* be read from beginning to end but may not be. However, a scientific document is rarely written from beginning to end. There are those who write from the first to the last sentence, but this is unusual. Our brains are capable of visualizing complex linkages and abstract connections. The written word, however, is linear. The linear structure of the written word is often limiting when trying to explain complex interactions. The outline is an effective tool to create a logical train of thought on a complex idea.

PARAGRAPH

Just like document structure, paragraph structure contains the organization of content in a logical order. Unlike document structure, however, paragraph structure is not an abstraction or a framework of the ideas. A paragraph contains the whole message. The whole message starts with the topic sentence.

A topic sentence should be the first sentence of a paragraph and contain its message. The message is then supported by subsequent sentences in the paragraph. Unlike a document that can be read out of order, paragraphs are read from beginning to end. When reading, you read the first sentence of a paragraph, assume it is the topic of the paragraph, and settle into that idea. When the topic wanders away from the first sentence, the reader's train of thought also wanders away. Placing the topic sentence in the middle or at the end of a paragraph simply leads to confusion. The reader wonders why you are saying these things and is unable to figure out that the sentence in the middle or end is the main topic. There is no opportunity to say to the reader, "Wait, wait, I'll get to the point soon; you just need to know these few things before I tell you the point." That does not work. You need to tell them the point of the paragraph in the topic sentence and then support the topic sentence with the remainder of the paragraph.

The sentences in the remainder of the paragraph need to follow the content and structure of the topic sentence they support. That means the content of the supporting sentences must not wander away from that found in the topic sentence. No new major theme should be introduced. Likewise, the structure of the topic sentence also needs to be followed. For example, when two ideas are introduced in the topic sentence, two ideas need to be supported in the remainder of the paragraph.

Paragraph structure can follow several formats, both correct and incorrect, illustrated in Figure 6.2. Figures 6.2a–c represent effective paragraph structure because the content supports the topic sentence. Figure 6.2a shows a paragraph with a topic sentence containing parallel structure (discussed in the Grammar section that follows). The remaining sentences of that paragraph reflect the same parallel structure, each with the same level of detail. Figure 6.2b has a topic sentence with a single idea. The remaining sentences support that single idea with specificity, elaboration, details, and explanation. The third effective paragraph structure is illustrated in Figure 6.2c. In this case, the topic sentence is a fairly general statement, and the remainder of the paragraph fine-tunes the general statement with increasing specificity. This third example, however, is the weakest of the effective structures. It is mostly used when linkages between paragraphs need to be made.

Figures 6.2 d–f show ineffective paragraph structures. Figure 6.2d starts with a solid topic sentence, but the remaining sentences wander off topic. The reader is confused by the introduction of the new subject, which remains unsupported. Figure 6.2e also illustrates a solid topic sentence, but the remainder of the paragraph broadens to a more general topic. This is ineffective because the reader expects more detail, not less. Figure 6.2f illustrates the wandering paragraph. The topic sentence is in the middle of the paragraph, and other sentences are either linked or not to the topic.

The last paragraph of this section, which describes the last two rules for paragraph structure, is an example of Figure 6.2a—the parallel structure. The topic sentence states there are two parallel items the paragraph will discuss. The next five sentences support the first of the two elements in the parallel structure. The next five sentences support the second of the two elements in the parallel structure. The fact that the two items in the topic sentence are described with similar level of detail (i.e., three and then four sentences) tells the reader they have the same level of importance.

Figure 6.2   Effective (a–c) and ineffective (d–f) paragraph structure with reference to a topic sentence. The blocks indicate sentences or groups of sentences; the dashed lines illustrate the boundaries of the topic. a) parallel structure; b) single idea supported; c) a general idea that leads to a specific idea; d) wandering paragraph that goes outside the theme of the topic sentence; e) a specific idea that leads to a general idea; f) rambling paragraph.

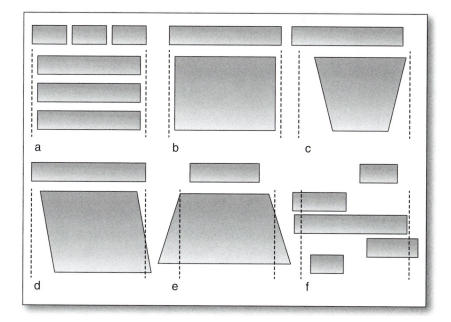

The previous paragraph is an example of Figure 6.2b—a single idea supported. The single idea described is an example of parallel structure. It is supported by the remaining sentences in the paragraph. These sentences support the single idea by elaborating on what constitutes a parallel-structured paragraph.

The final two rules for paragraph structure are simple. First, there should never be a one-sentence paragraph. A paragraph consists of a topic sentence and supporting sentences. A single-sentence paragraph lacks necessary support. As a rule of thumb, the minimum number is three sentences. However, a few more is better. The second rule is to eliminate all multiple-page paragraphs. A paragraph is a single idea (i.e., the topic sentence) and supporting information (the remaining sentences). A paragraph that spans multiple pages contains more than one idea. Typical paragraphs should have from 100 to 150 words. For example, this paragraph contains 102 words.

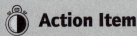 **Action Item**

Identify a section in the journal article you selected that has three to four paragraphs. In the margins of the paper, identify the paragraph structure using the terminology identified in Figure 6.2. Alternatively, if you identify a paragraph structure not included here, create new terminology that describes this form.

SENTENCE

The third structural component to evaluate is sentence structure. Remember that each sentence supports the paragraph structure with unique content. A sentence is either a topic sentence or a supporting sentence of the paragraph. In either case, it must contain content—a specific idea that contributes to the point of the paragraph. Sentences with redundancy from previous sentences use unnecessary space and waste the reader's attention.

While excessive redundancy is unacceptable, controlled redundancy is mandatory. Controlled redundancy is a deliberate link from one sentence to the next to maintain the flow of ideas. Diagrammatically, this link is visualized in Figure 6.3. As Figure 6.3 shows, there is overlap—often using identical words—from one sentence to the next. Beginning writers need to write overlapping sentences from the end of one sentence to the beginning of the next (see Figure 6.3a and Figure 6.3b). More advanced writers can sneak in the overlap in more subtle ways (Figure 6.3c).

The linkage between sentences is mandatory both internally within a paragraph as well as externally from the last sentence of a paragraph to the beginning of the next paragraph within a section. Internally, the linkage focuses the reader from one idea to the next. It shows the reader how the ideas are connected. Similarly, external linkages show how ideas are connected but from one paragraph to the next. The external linkages occur however only within a single section of the document.

Just like with document and paragraph structure, you can create sentence templates from other published works and identify the form from Figure 6.3. Graff, Birkenstein, and Durst (2011) use this approach to introduce how to develop your own arguments. Using templates is particularly effective in the literature review and methods sections. However, there may be a fine line between developing and using templates and plagiarism (see Chapter 2 on ethics in academia). The key to using templates is to keep the framework (or structure) of the sentence but incorporate your own ideas.

The following paragraph from Glick and Hohmann-Marriott (2007) is an example of a sentence structure illustrated in Figure 6.3b. The first two sentences begin with the word *view* (highlighted), tying a general idea in sentence one with a specific example in sentence two. The third sentence is linked to the second by having *this story* refer to the idea presented in the previous sentence. This is similar to Figure 3c.

Figure 6.3   The ovals represent controlled redundancy between sentences that link together ideas. a) links one idea to the next with overlapping structure from the end of one sentence to the beginning of the next; b) two adjacent sentences with the same subject at the beginning of the sentence; c) controlled redundancy between two sentences.

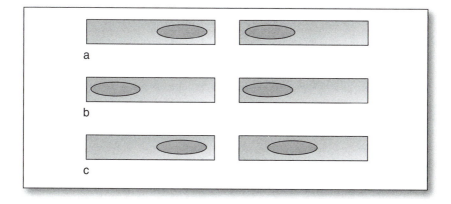

> One view is that that [*sic*] these children are appropriately compared to the majority (i.e., non-Hispanic White) children so that their adaptation to the American mainstream (e.g., their "assimilation") can be assessed. This classic, linear view suggests children from immigrant families may start out behind their peers with U.S.-born parents but that over time, through the socialization they receive in American schools, these children of immigrants catch up. In the case of the "model minority" stereotype applied to recent Asian migrants, this story may become even more dramatic if children of immigrants surpass their native peers (Kao, 1995).
>
> (Glick & Hohmann-Marriott, 2007, p. 372)

The first sentence from the Glick and Hohmann-Marriott's text can be converted into a template describing a view:

> One view is that _____ is/are [underline]adverb[/underline] compared to _____ (i.e., _____) so that _____ (e.g., their "_____") can be _____.

Using that sentence as a template, I can express an idea about writing.

> One view is that <u>structure</u> is <u>potentially</u> compared to <u>a jigsaw puzzle</u> (i.e., <u>pieces that fit together in a certain way to create an image</u>) so that <u>becoming an academic writer</u> (e.g., <u>a professor</u>) can be <u>fun</u>.

Creating and using writing templates is helpful but also a potentially dangerous and slippery slope toward unethical writing: plagiarism. Plagiarism, discussed more extensively in Chapter 2, refers to representing someone else's work (and words) as your own. Because of the Internet, other digital sources, and the copy/paste function, plagiarism is easier than ever. The temptation to simply "lift" an effectively worded idea may be appealing, but the long-term consequences are severe (e.g., dismissal from a graduate program, job loss). In the example just given, the presentation of the sentence (the template) is used and *not* the content.

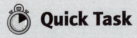

Quick Task

Return to the manuscript you selected to examine how effectively (or not) the author has linked sentences and paragraphs together. Do you see this pattern?

Grammar

The third item in the toolbox is grammar. Grammar refers to the rules on how to compose a sentence from a set of words. The rules govern areas like subject-verb agreement, verb tense, clauses, and word choices. Using these rules correctly will improve your writing clarity.

In addition to the ideas presented here, word processors and online grammar check systems offer assistance with evaluating grammatical rules. Furthermore, numerous books exist on grammar. Strunk and White's *The Elements of Style* (1999), first published in 1918, is a classic book on writing and a favorite among academics. The efforts in this section are not intended to replace or compete with any of these sources. The objective here is to provide guidance on what I frequently encounter with graduate students and their grammatical challenges. These are readily identified situations and can improve overall writing.

VERBS

Subject-verb agreement is the relationship between the verb form and the plurality or singularity of the subject. Most word processing software packages have a grammar check that performs a reasonable analysis of subject-verb agreement. There are, however, exceptions to what some software systems accept or reject. In particular, the word *data* is a plural subject and should have a plural verb form. For example, the correct form is "The data were collected." *Data*, however, is commonly used as single subject in many published documents. When publishing, consult with the editor on the correct form.

Deciding on verb tense—past, present, future—can be tricky for new authors. There are some simple guidelines that can be generally followed. Most sections of a proposal or paper can be written in the present tense. However, a proposal is something you *will* do, hence something in the future. This is particularly true of the methods section. It is written in the future tense because you are describing what you will do. This is in contrast to a journal article where the methods are typically written in the past tense because they describe something completed.

The literature review is tricky because it describes both what someone else has done (past tense) and your interpretation of this relative to the overall body of literature (present tense). The sentences describing other work are in the past tense because they describe work done already. The author *found* results and *reported* on those results in the literature. Both of these are in the past tense. Nevertheless, a critical analysis of the literature, which is your ideas, needs to be described in the present tense. You describe in the present tense how findings from different papers relate to one another.

Conclusions typically summarize the current work and suggest future avenues of research. This means they are potentially a combination of past, present, and future tenses. When writing, think about the structure of the paragraphs so the reader is not confused about when something was done.

PASSIVE VOICE

Books on writing suggest you minimize the passive voice. The reason is to make your writing more clear and direct. The passive voice is a form of sentence construction where the subject of the sentence *receives* the action. This is in contrast to an active voice where the subject of the sentence *does* the action. The active voice is clearer writing because who or what performed the action is identified. For example, the follow example could appear in a dissertation proposal:

> The dissertation project is expected to be completed in the next year. (Passive)

In this case, who is doing the dissertation is unclear. Here is the sentence revised into an active voice:

> I expect to complete the dissertation project in the next year. (Active, where the first person "I" refers to the author, the graduate student)

Using active language encourages the use of the first person, although that is not the only method to change a sentence from a passive structure.

Mindell (2001) agrees that authors and speakers should use the active voice in writing *and* speaking. In fact, she emphasizes that the passive voice is weak because of wordiness and opacity of form. However, she does suggest using the passive voice when you explicitly want to be unclear. This is particularly true in spoken language when the message is unpleasant.

VOCABULARY

This section contains simple reminders of sentence structures and word choices. The list features mistakes commonly found in graduate student writing. If the reminders are unfamiliar, refer to a grammar book (or look online) for a quick lesson.

1. Either define or avoid excessive use of jargon.

2. Do not end sentences with prepositions (e.g., *with, of, in*).

3. Eliminate use of all contractions (e.g., *can't, won't*).

4. Minimize the number of sentences that start with conjunctions (e.g., *and, but*).

5. Know how to use words correctly; e.g.,   *their, there,* and *they're*

   your and *you're*

   its and *it's*

   which and *that*

   compliment and *complement.*

6. Use *i.e.* (in other words) and *e.g.* (for example) correctly.

7. Avoid using *etc.*

8. Avoid using *get.*

PARALLEL STRUCTURE

Parallel structure is a powerful and effective form of communication requiring a consistent pattern and balance to be effective. *Pattern* refers to consistent grammatical form of the elements within a list of a sentence. Each element in the list has the same grammatical type, such as noun, adjective, adverb, phrase, or clause. For example, the previous sentence contains parallel structure with a list of nouns. The list can be as short as two items, but an excessively long list is unwise. A sentence with parallel structure also presents the subsequent supporting material in *balance* with the sentence. This means the number of sentences or paragraphs to support each item in the list should be roughly the same. If this is not possible, then the parallel structure needs to be reconsidered. Details on both pattern and balance follow.

Pattern

A key element to writing successful sentences with a parallel structure is to keep the same grammatical form throughout a list. If a list contains adverbs, then the whole list must be adverbs. Likewise, if the pattern is phrases, the phrases need to have the same grammatical form. For example, the following examples show incorrect followed by correct usage of parallel structure:

1. She enjoyed Saturdays because she likes biking, cooking, and friends. (Poor parallel form)

2. She enjoyed Saturdays because she likes biking, cooking, and spending time with friends. (Correct form but unbalanced)

3. She enjoyed Saturdays because she likes biking with her children, cooking for her family, and spending time with friends. (Correct and balanced)

The first sentence is poor because the third item on the list, "friends," is not in the present progressive verb tense. This weakens the reader's understanding of the sentence. The sentence can be reworded so that all three are in the same verb tense. Sentence 2 fulfills this requirement by creating a better parallel form. However, the last item on the list, "spending time with friends," is a phrase, making the pattern unbalanced. The last sentence (3) is the best form because the pattern is consistent (all the same verb tense) and balanced (all three items in the list are phrases).

A topic sentence with parallel structure is strong because it identifies content for the topic sentence and provides the structure for the remaining paragraph. The content identified in the topic sentence is then elaborated on with details in the remainder of the paragraph. The details provide the supporting information needed for the topic sentence. The structure, or order of the details, needs to be the same as was stated in the topic sentence. This keeps the reader from being confused as the sentence unfolds.

Balance

The content following and supporting the parallel structure needs to be balanced. Balance here means the same level of detail, defined by the number of phrases, sentences, or paragraphs. For example, the introductory paragraph of a section may introduce three ideas. The remaining paragraphs then define those ideas relative to your research topic. Each of those descriptive paragraphs should be roughly the same length because they are considered equally important. The same is true when a topic sentence is constructed with parallel structure. The remainder of the paragraph elaborates on each item in the list, in the order presented. If the first item has two supporting sentences, then so should the second one. For example, the following is a paragraph from this section:

> Parallel structure is a powerful and effective form of communication requiring a consistent <u>pattern</u> and <u>balance</u> to be effective. _Pattern_ <u>refers to consistent grammatical form of the elements within a list of a sentence. Each element in the list has the same grammatical type, such as noun, adjective, adverb, phrase, or clause. For example, the previous sentence contains parallel structure with a list of nouns. The list can be as short as two items, but an excessively long list is unwise.</u>
>
> <u>A sentence with parallel structure also presents the subsequent supporting material in _balance_ with the sentence. This means the number of sentences or paragraphs to support each item in the list should be roughly the same. If this is not possible, then the parallel structure needs to be reconsidered. Details on both pattern and balance follow.</u>

The topic sentence contains parallel structure with two elements: pattern and balance. This pattern of the parallel structure is two nouns. The balance in the remainder of the paragraph is four sentences per item in the list. The parallel structure is maintained through the rest of the section. Pattern (described in detail first) is supported by two paragraphs and one example. Likewise, balance (described in detail second) is also supported by two paragraphs and one example. The reader is clear that both pattern and balance are important.

The parallel structure in a sentence is an indication that each element receives the same level of importance. Even though the ideas are presented in a particular order, there is no implied emphasis. This is an important tool because if you recall, our thoughts and ideas are not linear but writing is. The parallel structure utilizes a linear mechanism for conveying ideas and translates them into a holistic and multifaceted understanding of your thoughts. Even the outline of your document is a form of parallel structure. Each section is equally important.

 Action Item

1. Skim the manuscript you selected and find examples of parallel structure. Highlight or underline them and note whether they do or do not use the method correctly.
   a. Look for whether or not the pattern is consistent.
   b. Look at whether the subsequent material follows the parallel structure.

2. Create a template with parallel structure.

3. Skim a paper you wrote. Look for correct and incorrect parallel structure. Fix any incorrect patterns or balance.

AUTOMATIC GRAMMAR CHECK

Whether to use the automatic grammar check in word processing software is a very good question. In the spelling corrections, make sure the suggested word is the word you intend it to be and that the language setting is correct (e.g., British versus American English). Sometimes, grammar-checking suggestions will rearrange a sentence into something that loses the intended meaning. However, grammar check software rarely identifies problems with parallel structure construction. When the grammar check highlights something, review the sentence and decide for yourself what it should be instead of simply accepting the default suggestion.

Document Format

A simple but important tool in the toolbox is the document format. Format is the physical appearance of the manuscript. Universities provide students with guidelines on how to format a thesis or dissertation, and departments or advisors may also have similar guidelines for the proposal. Document format includes the page length, margins, font style, and font size. Also critical are table structure (e.g., borders and shading) and figure composition (e.g., color or black and white). The guidelines indicate how to reference tables, figures, and equations. They may tell you whether to use the symbol % or write out the word *percent*. There are also specific guidelines on formatting section headings (numbering format, font format) and on formatting citations within the document and reference section. All formatting must be consistent through the document.

Publishers and granting agencies also provide guidelines to authors on how a document should be formatted. Each and every guideline must be followed precisely. This is out of respect for the publisher or granting agency but also to expedite your publishing or funding prospects. For example, granting agencies *reject without review* a proposal with incorrect formatting. This is a massive blow to scholars who put considerable effort into writing a proposal. A proposal with a smaller-than-required font size and pages with narrower margins will have a higher word count compared to proposals with the correct format. This gives an unfair advantage to the incorrectly formatted proposal because competing proposals will have fewer words to explain their message.

 Action Item

1. Go to the graduate college website of your university and read their requirements for theses and dissertations. Start using them now.

2. Obtain the guidelines for prospective authors for a leading journal in your field. The guidelines are found either in a hard copy of the journal (often at the end) or on the journal's website. Read the guidelines and note the level of detail.

Revise and Resubmit

As most seasoned authors know, writing is not about the first words but going back through (typically several times) and rewriting them. Authors, advisors, editors, publishers, and granting agencies use the phrase "revise and resubmit" or R&R to denote the idea that a manuscript or grant proposal *as is* is not yet ready for publication or funding. It means there is potential for publication or a grant because of a good idea, an excellent dataset, or a compelling solution.

Writing a proposal and eventually a dissertation likewise is an iterative process. While the student does the work, the advisor and the committee members support the research and the writing. They provide feedback on how to improve the document. Feedback from an advisor or committee member is not a directive to start over but to revise, recast, rewrite, and reevaluate.

The revision process exists during graduate school and throughout an academic career. Few authors can write a perfect paper the first time through. What is required instead is the commitment to put something down the first time and the willingness to change it later to say what you really mean in a way that conveys your ideas. The first sentences you write are not final—they start out as ideas (the content). Revisions come later (the presentation).

There are two steps to the revision process: getting feedback and making changes based on that feedback. Getting feedback means someone else (or you) reads the manuscript and, with knowledge on the prospective audience, provides constructive commentary on how to improve it. Making changes means addressing the constructive feedback through rewriting the document's content or presentation. Learning to read, interpret, and revise based on feedback is key.

Rewriting involves evaluating and responding to feedback. This section describes how to provide feedback to someone else, how to receive feedback from yourself or someone else, and how to interpret feedback. The process of giving and receiving feedback is constant in an academic career from a graduate student to a senior scholar.

GIVE FEEDBACK

The first lesson in understanding how to interpret feedback is to learn how to give it constructively. The goal is to provide constructive (useful, practical, helpful) information to an author so the document can be improved. This lesson improves your ability to recognize good and effective feedback relative to unhelpful and unkind feedback.

Feedback is like any written document; it requires content and presentation. The content of feedback needs two elements: strengths and weaknesses. Some journal publishers and grant agencies require this. Strengths indicate to authors what is right or interesting or relevant about the work. Weaknesses tell authors what needs to be improved. The presentation of your feedback needs to include both strengths and weaknesses (even if the weaknesses section dominates what you write). Start with a sentence or two that describes, in your own words, the objective or goals of the document. Typically this is considered a strength of the document, but your presentation of it should be an interpretation of what authors are doing without any consideration of it as a strength or weakness. Second, write a section describing the strengths of the document as is. It could be that the document is well written, the graphics are effective, the methods are robust, or anything else done well. Third, write a section that addresses major and minor concerns. The major concerns could be on the content, the presentation, or both. Conclude with a section on minor comments. These are typically on the presentation of the work rather than on the content. Give this feedback to the author.

SELF-FEEDBACK

Beginning in primary school, we are instructed to proofread our work. It is difficult, however, to read your own words from an objective point of view. The task is to read your own words as if they are *not* your words (so you do not make assumptions about what is said) and think about what a reader would understand. It is more difficult to master this than reading and providing feedback on other people's work. Start to develop this skill by reading something you wrote a few months ago rather than something you wrote recently. Giving yourself time to forget what you meant rather than what you actually wrote provides perspective.

Be honest with yourself. Actually read the words and think about what they say rather than what you meant. It helps to read sections out loud. Answer these questions: Does what you say sound right? Does it make sense? What do the words really say?

EXTERNAL FEEDBACK

One of the most difficult moments in graduate school is the first time a student has a significant manuscript returned from a professor or the editor of a journal. Unlike an undergraduate who has less emotional and intellectual investment in a term paper, graduate students make huge investments in manuscripts. The feedback can be shocking and disappointing. Responses include anger, frustration, embarrassment, and fear. Some students have gone as far to say, "Should I consider a different career?" The answer is no. Critical feedback is normal.

The key to receiving feedback (and eventually responding to it) is to not take comments personally. Despite the personal investment, comments are not about you as a person. What are the worst possible comments a reviewer might say that could cause you fear or anger? What is a less emotional response to that feedback? Table 6.1 includes several typical reviewer comments, the emotional response to those comments, and an alternative response to better deal with the comment.

Comments like those in Table 6.1 can be handled during a rewrite. Move past the emotional response and figure out why the reviewer made a statement. Most reviewers (and certainly most advisors) provide feedback to be helpful. There are instances, however, where the commentary is sarcastic, a personal attack, or an attempt to undermine your work. If you suspect that reviewer feedback is anything but constructive, speak with your advisor or the editor about it.

The book *Writing for Social Scientists: How to Start and Finish Your Thesis, Book, or Article* by Howard S. Becker emphasizes the need to rewrite and the emotional factors in writing. In fact, these are among the central theses of his book. He elaborates on these themes by showing the challenges of writing, copyediting, and rewriting.

RESPONDING TO FEEDBACK

Being successful in rewriting is recognizing it is not the reader's responsibility to understand what the author means; instead, it is the author's responsibility to write what is meant. Feedback gives you insight into how a reader interprets the writing. Responding to feedback requires analyzing a comment and figuring out what the reviewer meant by it. Why did he or she come to that conclusion when reading that section, paragraph, or sentence? Try to figure out if the reviewer disagreed with the message—the content—or if it is the way something was said—the presentation. When comments are about presentation, simply change it according to the reviewer's suggestion if appropriate. In the case of content, you need to decide if you agree or disagree with the reviewer and make a change based on that principle. The trickiest instance is when the comment appears to be about the content but in reality is about the presentation. In those cases, the paragraph or sentence just does not express your idea in the way you intended it. The idea is in your head the way reviewer expected but not the way you actually stated it. Responding to this requires a deeper ability to read what you actually wrote (and not just meant) and changing it.

Feedback comes in many flavors. Some reviewers are specific and others vague. Table 6.2 and Table 6.3 list some general types of feedback (with less emotion than those in Table 6.1) followed by the interpretation and possible action.

For each of these, the author can then look closely at the sentence, paragraph, or document and fix the problem. Some are quick fixes and some take time. Even with those that take time, the investment is worthwhile.

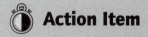

Action Item

Give and receive feedback with graduate students in your program. Exchange (for example) the AOS statement you wrote as part of Chapter 4. Ask one or two students to read and comment on it. Take those suggestions and improve your writing.

Table 6.1 Common emotional responses to feedback on writing and alternative responses.

Comment	Emotional Response	Alternative Response
Clearly the author has no knowledge of the subject matter.	Ouch! Hurtful.	Learn more about your subject matter. Use references.
X has done this work before; there is no new contribution here.	Frustration! I want to quit!	Look carefully at the work by X. There will be differences between that work and yours. Identify them.
This is poorly written.	Anger! The reviewer just didn't know what I meant.	Read it from a reviewer's perspective. It is incumbent on the author to say precisely what is meant.
The data were incorrectly analyzed; assumptions were not met; interpretation was wrong.	Fear and panic. Do I have to start over? I don't have time for this!	Take the time needed to learn about your data and the method you use. Use references to clarify your assumptions.

Other Challenges

For some, writing is fun and relaxing, for others it is challenging but exciting, and for some it is difficult and painful. The reason can relate to the topic or level of experience. This section focuses on two challenges: writer's block and English as a second language.

WRITER'S BLOCK

Writer's block is a myth and simply an excuse for not writing. Everyone may feel it from time to time, but it needs to be overcome. Someone experiencing writer's block is stumped for a specific reason. Similarly, you do not have to be in the "mood" to write. The mood aspect is another form of procrastination. Three things help: figuring out the problem, doing more than writing, and writing every day.

Table 6.2   How to deal with specific types of feedback on the content.

Content	
Comment	**Action**
Key knowledge is missing from the background or literature review.	Update the literature review with suggested references.
Key elements are incorrect or inaccurately presented.	Review the key elements; determine if you were wrong and revise. If you were not wrong, determine what in the text led the reviewer to interpret it this way.
Justification is needed for the study area or data collection methods.	Provide justification.
Methods are not appropriate for the data; key assumptions are not met.	Review the methods and determine the assumptions. If the assumptions were unmet, you may need to redo the analysis with different methods.
The interpretation of the results is not derived from the data presented.	Read your results interpretation and compare it to your data; make the connection clear and obvious.
Formulas or models were not accurately implemented.	Go to a reliable source (not Wikipedia) to understand the model implementation. Follow it and cite the source.
There is no new knowledge presented.	Understand why the reviewer said this; was it based on something you said earlier (the contribution will be X and you never delivered it)? Make a clear statement by saying, "The contribution of this . . ."

Table 6.3   How to deal with specific feedback on the presentation or writing.

Presentation	
Comment	**Action**
Unnecessary background material is included.	Synthesize, shorten, or delete sections.
What is the point of this paragraph?	Look at the topic sentence. Make sure each sentence in the paragraph supports the topic sentence.

(Continued)

Table 6.3   (Continued)

Presentation	
Comment	**Action**
The logic isn't here.	Read all topic sentences and outline the logic.
Poor grammar.	Read a grammar rules book. It is likely you broke one or two "pet" rules of the reviewer.
Inconsistency in terminology, style, or phrasing.	Watch the use of synonyms in key terms of your work. Use the search function in the word processor to verify the systematic use.

For most cases, writer's block occurs because of procrastination. Here are some possible scenarios that may cause you to feel writer's block:

1. You are writing about a difficult subject matter that requires extensive reading. You feel pressure to write and are nervous or anxious about taking time to read when you feel you just need to write. Take the time to read and remember to use active reading to make the writing more efficient.

2. The content may be unclear to you because you have not finished analyzing your data or interpreting your results.

3. You have comments from a committee member that you do not understand or know how to address. Addressing them seems like it will take *forever* and you have a deadline. Speak with the committee member or your advisor about how to address the problem. Sometimes the issue may be easier than you think.

4. You know you need to restructure a paper, but the major revision will just take so much time. In this case, return to the outline to see the big picture. Take time to move the pieces into the right organization.

5. Sometimes writer's block (or the feeling of it) occurs because you are trying to write well and just do not know how to say it just right. In this case, write down your thoughts and save the "right words" for the revision.

6. Sometimes you are trying to write a section (e.g., the introduction) when you do not know what to say. Instead, start writing a different section, such as the literature review or the methods. Finalize the writing with the introduction and conclusion. This method helps maintain the feedback linkages as illustrated in Figure 6.1. A paper does not need to be written from the beginning to the end. Even readers may not approach it this way.

If you find you are unable to write, take time to dig down into your thoughts and find the reason why. Figure out if you are distracted by other things (or worries) or unsure about the subject or your message. It can also be because the material is just plain difficult. Regardless of the problem, once you identify it, you can move past the feeling of writer's block and continue to write.

Recognize that writing is more than putting down new words. Writing involves reading, taking notes, reviewing others' work, revising, and engaging with colleagues. If you are stumped, allow yourself to find alternatives to writing that will stimulate you into putting new words down.

Writing is something that must take place every day. It becomes a habit and part of the research process—from investigating the topic, to writing the proposal, collecting data, analyzing data, interpreting results, and disseminating results. You are writing (or taking notes) all the time on what you are doing. Writing is not performed as the end task but as the medium for dissemination. *How to Write a Lot* by Paul Silva (2007) provides numerous ideas on how to write every day. It starts with picking a time to write and committing to that time.

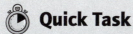

🕐 Quick Task

Commit to writing every day. Start with a 30-minute block of time and gradually increase it to 2 hours.

ENGLISH AS A SECOND LANGUAGE

While everyone may feel writer's block, writing in English when it is your second language is another challenge (ESL). If English is not your first language and you are in academia, you will need to learn to write (and read and speak) fluently in English. This is true whether you plan on residing in an English-speaking country or not. Many international journals are published in English and many international conferences are held in English. International scholars all write and speak effectively in English.

The first rule is to avoid the temptation to use automated translators. These work in a pinch—for example, to read a phrase or understand a word—but they should not be used for writing. Typically, these translators are effective at converting the main message but do so using awkward language. Learn instead to think and write in the language.

The second rule is to seek assistance. Most large universities have writing centers that cater to graduate students and in particular to foreign graduate students. Seek out these services early in your studies instead of waiting until you are writing your dissertation. If this guidance is not enough, there are professional editing services that specialize in academic writing. Some include Edanz Editing, International Science Editing, and SPI Publisher Services.

There is a fee associated with these services, but you may be able to negotiate a student rate.

The third piece of advice is to read novels in English. The best source is fiction for young adults, which you can find at the local public library. These sources will improve your reading and writing skills in ways that academic writing (e.g., nonfiction or journal articles) do not. They demonstrate the fluidity in the language, nuances, and exceptions to grammatical rules. Such books will broaden the ESL student's vocabulary and ability to express ideas.

Reminders

- Use the toolbox for self-feedback: content, structure, grammar, and format.
- Topic sentences relay the message of the paragraph.
- Sentences need to be linked.
- Paragraphs need to be linked.
- The document needs to flow logically from one section to the next.
- Seek feedback and revise.
- Write every day.

References

Becker, H. S. (2007). *Writing for social scientists: How to start and finish your thesis, book, or article* (2nd ed.). Chicago: University of Chicago Press.

Creswell, J. W. (2009). *Research design: Qualitative, quantitative, and mixed methods approaches* (3rd ed.). Thousand Oaks, CA: Sage.

Glick, J., & Hohmann-Marriott, B. (2007). Academic performance of young children in immigrant families: The significance of race, ethnicity, and national origins. *International Migration Review, 41*(2), 371–402. doi:10.1111/j.1747-7379.2007.00072.x

Graff, G., Birkenstein, C., & Durst, R. (2011). *"They Say/I Say." The moves that matter in academic writing with readings* (2nd ed.). New York: W. W. Norton.

Mindell, P. (2001). *How to say it for women: Communicating with confidence and power using the language of success.* Upper Saddle River, NJ: Prentice Hall.

Silva, P. (2007). *How to write a lot: A practical guide to productive academic writing.* Washington, DC: American Psychological Association.

Strunk Jr., W., & White, E. B. (1999). *The elements of style* (4th ed.). Boston: Allyn & Bacon.

7

The Literature Review

Introduction

Chapter 4 describes how to write the area of specialization (AOS Statement). The AOS document defines the area you consider your specialty and describes the major research themes within. The literature review starts where the AOS left off and digs deeper into those themes by discussing what is known about your particular area, identifying the methods used to investigate those themes, and highlighting what remains unknown.

A literature review is a synthesis (not a summary) of previous work in a specific area(s). A synthesis means you are bringing together different aspects of the literature and creating something new with it. The result is a critical evaluation of the current theory and methods of a particular topic reflecting what is known, how it is known, and what is unknown. The objective of the literature review in a proposal is to provide the reader with the knowledge needed to understand your proposal. It is not an explanation of everything you know about a particular subject. Because of this distinction, you need to perform a thorough investigation of the literature but synthesize only the material *relevant* to your proposed research.

A literature review relevant to the reader is written twice during the proposal writing process. The difference, as illustrated in Figure 7.1, is the topical breadth of each revision. The first version is a comprehensive review of the literature with the objective of teaching yourself what is known about your interest area. The goal is to broadly learn what has been done and what needs to be done. Your research questions emerge from this first stage. The second and final version is a focused review of the literature with the objective to inform the reader about what is known and unknown in your research area. The research area is a narrower set of literature based on the research questions developed. The outcome of this stage is included in the research proposal. I bring this up because of multiple discussions with students about where to begin the development of a proposal. Some students argue that the process should begin with the research question so they know what literature to examine. While this is true for the second stage, it is at the first stage where the research questions emerge. Begin the proposal with the literature.

The literature review is a synthesis of prior research. Synthesizing the literature means identifying and tying together key articles and themes. The linkages between key themes show the reader similarities or differences in points of view on particular topics. The synthesis approach is in contrast to a literature summary. A literature summary (or annotated bibliography) provides a brief statement on individual articles without linking them to each other. If you find that each paragraph of the literature review summarizes a single article, it is an indication you are probably doing a summary instead of a review.

Writing a literature review can be a daunting task for students. Students ask how many articles they should cite. It depends. Other students ask how many pages the literature review should be. Again, the answer is that it depends. Mostly it depends on discipline traditions or university-specific rules that guide the format and length of the whole proposal, of which the literature review is a portion. Some general guidelines for a research proposal suggest that 5 to 10 reference articles probably is not enough and 200+ is probably too many. Likewise, one to two pages of text for the literature review portion is not

Figure 7.1   Spiral showing the two levels of a literature review.

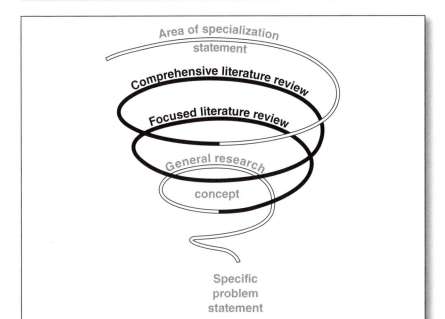

enough and 50+ is probably too many. Writing and deciding the scope of the literature review is therefore complicated. Because of that, the process of writing either paralyzes students and they never start, or the amount of literature seems endless and they never know when or how to stop. The concrete steps described here will help students start, move through, and complete the process of writing a literature review.

Theoretical Framework

Most students will eventually hear the question, "What is the theoretical framework for your research?" Be ahead of the game and have an answer prepared. The basic idea of a theoretical framework is that it is a guiding principle for research that provides structure or an explanation to a problem. It represents how an investigator considers, formulates, and solves a problem. The idea of a theoretical framework is introduced now because as you examine the literature, you want to build your own guiding principles by identifying those that exist in the literature. A meta-objective of the literature review is to identify and define a theoretical framework for your own research.

A theory describes the best-known explanation for the nature and causes of a phenomenon. The nature of a phenomenon is the characteristics of it or the features that make it what it is. The causes are what drive the phenomenon to change or become what it is. In a positivist reference, a theory is verified or falsified through empirical evidence or support. Some famous scientific theories are the Big Bang theory (creation of the universe), plate tectonics (Earth's continent and ocean arrangement), and the theory of evolution (how inheritance passes from one living generation to the next). In the social sciences, some well-known theories are postmodernism, critical theory, and feminist theory, each providing a framework or structure to what characterizes or explains social phenomenon.

The rationale for associating the word *framework* with theory is because the theoretical framework is general rather than specific to the research problem. A framework is a structure providing the outline and organization for something with unknown specifics. A theoretical framework can provide the beginning point for an exploratory research process, showing the pattern and path to the emergence of a research question. The theoretical framework also helps the investigator and readers of the research document to understand the logic and assumptions inherent in the research.

Theories are used in scientific inquiry through either deductive or inductive reasoning. Both are forms of logical thinking used to learn and explain the world. Theory is either used as the starting point and conclusions about a selected group are identified (deduction), or observations about a group are the starting point and the theory is the conclusion (induction). As Figure 7.2 illustrates, theory emerges at either end of the logical process.

Figure 7.2   Deductive and inductive reasoning logic.

Deduction: Theory → Hypothesis → Observations → Conclusion

Induction: Observations → Hypothesis → Conclusion → Theory

In reality, most scientific investigations rely on an iterative relationship between deductive and inductive reasoning. This serves to use existing theory to draw conclusions (typically a theoretical framework) and to use observations to develop (and verify) theory.

Some investigators use *theoretical framework, conceptual framework,* and *paradigm* synonymously. While similar, these terms are not perfectly interchangeable. Unlike theoretical framework, a conceptual framework may or may not have *theory* associated with it. Instead it is an approach to solving a problem in a particular way. It is typically less strict than a theoretical framework because it may include empirical observations, untested or untestable hypotheses, and intuition. Using a conceptual framework, a theory or theoretical framework may emerge.

More broadly, a paradigm is a point of view on how groups of researchers have implicitly decided to investigate a particular aspect of the world. It is a useful construct because it allows investigators to make and use assumptions about a generally accepted approach to solving a problem or understanding a phenomenon. For example, a functionalist paradigm in sociology considers the functional role and interdependence of different parts of society to evaluate the stability of society as a whole. While there are functionalist-based theories, the functionalist paradigm alone is not a theory on how or why societies are stable. Instead, it provides an approach to develop theories.

A specific paradigm represents a general course of action on how research should be approached relative to epistemology, theories, and methods (Punch, 2006). There may be one or more theoretical and conceptual frameworks associated with a particular paradigm. The notion that paradigms "shift" suggests that the transition from one paradigm to another is not bounded and discrete but instead has overlapping characteristics. The epistemology associated with paradigms refers to the things we know and how we know them. While it is a debated point of view, Kuhn (1996) described science as a sequence of changing norms—paradigm shifts. Kuhn's premise was that as understanding of a phenomenon matures, the paradigm changes and new ones appear (Kuhn, 1996). While Kuhn argued there were no paradigms in the social sciences, some researchers now view, for example, critical theory and postmodernism as paradigms in the social sciences.

 Action Item

To the best of your ability now (prior to starting the literature review), answer these questions in just a few sentences:

What is the nature or character of your problem?

What approach to your problem may solve it?

At this point, I want to avoid specifically using the terms *research question* and *methods* because those will come later as detailed items emerge after the literature review.

Concrete Steps to Move Forward

The next activity in writing a research proposal is to use these abstract ideas on theory to read, comprehend, and write about the literature in your area. Here the approach can help you systematically tackle this interesting but daunting task. It may be time to refer back to your motivational images or phrases from Chapter 1 to stay strong. The approach to writing a literature review described here is not the only way to go, but this approach has been tested multiple times successfully. The focused literature review (Version 2), which is a refined synthesis relevant to your proposal, is covered in Chapter 12.

This approach for completing a comprehensive (Version 1) literature review has five meta-steps: 1) identify keywords and references, 2) create an annotated bibliography, 3) organize and synthesize, 4) write and rewrite, 5) review and revise. Each meta-step has two or more subsets (with repeats) that need to be completed.

1. IDENTIFY KEYWORDS AND REFERENCES

A. Return to your AOS and determine the major themes (most students have from two to four themes). Write three to five keywords per theme here: _____

_____

_____

_____

B. Using the keywords, perform an initial search of the literature using one of the citation indices described in Chapter 5 on reading. Create a bibliography that includes about 10 to 20 articles with about three to five per theme from your AOS. Select articles that seem to be the most well known in the field, the most recent, or the most relevant to your topic. These articles represent focused starting points along the extremities of the spiral (see Figure 7.3). Share this list with your advisor to verify you are starting in the right place. Here is why. If you plan to conduct research on the environmental consequences of different policies and you select East and West Germany in the 1970s as your study area, one primary focus of the literature review would be the environmental consequences of policy of contrasting governments. The major theme would not be the history of East and West Germany. While this information would be relevant (certainly to justify this as your study area), it is not the primary theme of your literature review.

C. After validating the themes and direction, go broad. Using the tools from the Finding the Material to Read section in Chapter 5 on effective reading skills, create a list of 50 to 80 articles for your themes. At this point, have the list contain references and the abstract instead of the full article. This activity represents finding the material that "fills the spaces between the dots" on the spiral so that the picture at this level is understood.

2. CREATE AN ANNOTATED BIBLIOGRAPHY

The annotated bibliography is a summary of articles. It describes what was investigated, what was found, and how it relates to your own research. Likewise, when discussing references, explain what the authors studied (e.g., bees) but also what they found (e.g., bees need pollen to make honey). Without the finding, knowing what they studied is meaningless to your story.

The following steps help build an annotated bibliography that forms the basis of the literature review.

Figure 7.3   Finding the key points within the comprehensive literature review level of the spiral.

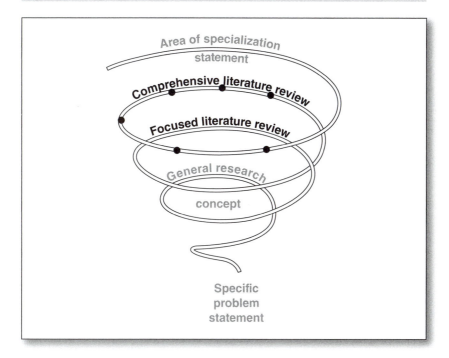

A. Create a database of articles. This step can take a long time, but each article should receive only a short amount of attention. Think triage. You can organize yourself systematically through referencing software or something as simple as a spreadsheet or word processing software (again, refer to Chapter 5). With your list, perform the following tasks:

- Create the following headings: author, year, title, journal, volume, pages, doi, priority, topic, methods, scope/study area, and findings (see Figure 7.4).
- Enter the articles from your initial list to the database; fill in all fields up to "priority." This step can be performed automatically by exporting the list of records from the citation index report.
- Read the abstract (and selected pieces of the article if necessary) to complete the record. Complete the remainder of the record for the article with the following guidelines:

   ○ Topic. What were they studying? This can be answered with a phrase or a few words.
   ○ Methods. What approach did they use? A few simple words should suffice to remind you of the work they did.

    ○ Scope/study area. Where was the research conducted? What were the characteristics of the focus group? This might relate to your work because then you can definitively say something like, "The research being proposed has never been examined in tropical cities."

    ○ Findings. What did the article you read contribute to the literature? This step is *critical* because it tells the reader what was learned that was unknown before. It is not enough to know that so-and-so studied bees using observational methods in Bangladesh. You also need to know they learned that the bees make brown and not yellow honey. This column will be critical as you construct your literature review. When you write this column use your own words so you do not accidently plagiarize the article.

    ○ Priority. Try using simple categories: high, medium, and low. You need to decide how central this reference is to your work. To have a thorough literature review, you need to reach just past the boundaries of your work to be certain you have covered everything in your own work. If you decide on "high" but only skimmed the reference, you may want to read it now or set it aside for active reading later.

- Read the list of references in each article. Identify new references you need to acquire. Add the title and journal information to the database before you have the article so you have a running list of articles that seem worthwhile. Another column in the database could even be "have article."

B. Using the database, write an annotated bibliography from the articles (not just the abstract). Some people do this in lieu of the database file because much of the information is reused or redundant. I find, however, that managing both is important. In part because this is where you need to read the articles, not just the abstract. Start with those high on the list—about 10% of the total list. For these, answer the following questions:

Figure 7.4   Sample empty database.

author	year	title	journal	vol/ pages	doi	priority	topic	methods	scope/ study area	findings

- The authors are studying _____.
- They found _____.
- The reason I read this article is _____.

In studying _____, Author et al. found that _____ relates to _____, but this was discovered without knowledge of _____.

In the annotated bibliography, write about their work in your own words. Again, this is critical to avoid accidental plagiarism as the annotated bibliography morphs into your literature review. Key to this step is translating what you are reading into something meaningful about your own work. Remember too that this is the *first* time you are writing the ideas. Worry about the content not the presentation.

Return to the list and repeat the process for the medium- and low-priority articles. Spend considerably less time with these but enough to understand the overall contribution.

    C. Return now to the literature. Obtain more relevant references from the citations found in articles you already read and from the articles identified as high priority. Also return to the library resources and use your keywords to acquire more articles. Repeat Step A and Step B with new references.

The challenge for many students is to decide when to stop repeating Steps A, B, and C. It can be overwhelming. There are several markers that tell you when to stop: when new articles are in obscure journals or conference proceedings and are difficult to acquire, when you start seeing the same articles appear in the list of references, when you list "low" on the priority column in your database more often than not, and when it just seems like you have a lot of material.

You can also identify the outer limit (and a reasonable stopping point) when you find an area that seems to have a flood of information—a Pandora's box. Unless that theme is central to your work, it is often sufficient to simply identify the area—recognize its existence—and move on. Because at some point, you need to say to yourself, "Stop, I have enough to start writing." Let yourself say *stop*.

3. ORGANIZE AND SYNTHESIZE

So far these steps can be accomplished with moderate thinking and concentration. The work up until now has been systematic and less creative. The next step requires deeper thinking and creativity, less systematic concentration, and more work. You want to figure out the story the literature tells. You can perform this either the old-fashioned way using paper and pen or the digital way, using mind-mapping software. Or even a little bit of both. If you have never used mind-mapping software, this is a good time to explore its functionality.

A. Tips for doing it the old-fashioned way. Creating piles . . .

- Print the author/title/abstract for your highly relevant articles.
- Either directly on the printout or on a Post-it note write the key contributions or theme of each article as it relates to your research.
- Create piles of articles with similar contributions.
- Sometimes (or often) a single article will fit into more than one pile, so make another copy of the author/title/abstract page and add it to the other pile.
- What emerges from this process are the major themes and what papers contribute to each theme.
- Repeat this process for the medium- and low-relevance articles. When you return, you may decide some of the references do not fit into any pile (or theme) and are not relevant. It is a good idea to weed out some of these now.

B. Tips for doing it the digital way (see Figure 7.5).

- Using your annotated bibliography, read each entry. You can start with the high-relevance articles or just work your way through the list.
- In your mind-mapping software, create nodes that represent the topic of the article. Use the child (and sibling) nodes to identify which articles support the topic and include here what each contributed.
- As you continue through the bibliography, link together articles as they contradict or complement one another (this is one of the major advantages over the paper and pen method) because you have to do the linking when you write.
- Like the paper and pen method, you will begin to see a pattern in nodes, including which ones have a lot of child nodes and their content.
- Use the resources the paper and pen method does not offer, such as the icons (e.g., the idea, the question, important), graphics, html, and formatting the objects. These tools help you develop the picture of the literature you need.

C. Examine the piles and/or nodes that emerge. These become your major themes. What do they represent? Can you organize these into a meaningful order, either chronologically (How did the prevailing understanding of your subject evolve?) or conceptually (What are the major problems addressed and solved?)?

D. If major themes do not naturally appear, you should probably go back through the literature, particularly articles labeled "high," and identify the methods used. You may include this in your literature or you may not. Either way, it is useful to know the approaches other researchers have successfully taken.

E. You may also find that you need to return to the literature for more articles to fill out or support what you have so far. That's okay—good even.

Don't kid yourself, Step 3 requires hard work. It takes concentration and can feel overwhelming. But if you approach it systematically with focus, then the major themes and patterns will emerge.

Figure 7.5 This illustrates how mind-mapping software can help organize your literature review. You can use icons such as the stop sign to identify areas of the literature that do not need further investigation. You can also use arrows to link ideas from one part of the organization to another. Documents and external links can be integrated. This example was taken from an open-source package called FreeMind.

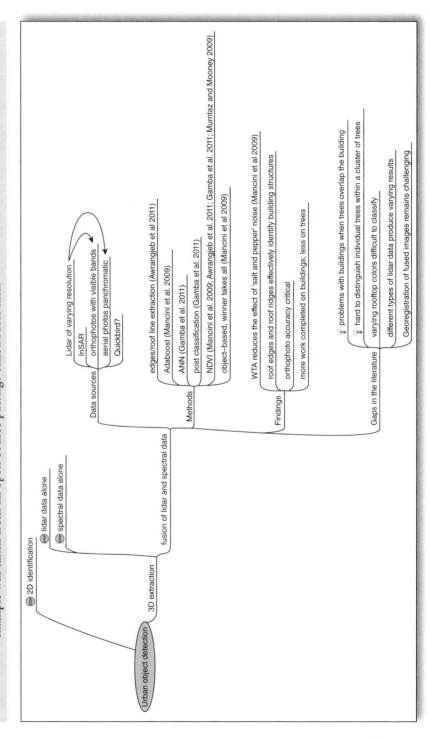

4. WRITE AND REWRITE

As stated in the beginning of this chapter, the literature review is a structured and critical examination of the literature *relevant* to the research you propose. At times, one of the challenges is deciding if something is relevant or not. You need to read more than just what is central to your work to determine the pieces that are truly relevant.

After reading extensively and writing an annotated bibliography the raw material exists to write a comprehensive literature review. The remaining job is to pull all of this material together into a coherent document. Instead of summarizing the literature, a literature review synthesizes the material into meaningful topics. Paragraphs need to be about topics and the details of the topics with key references. You will generate your own organization of topics and a critical evaluation of them. That way, the literature review you write supports your research by providing an argument that what you plan to do remains unknown. At this stage, remember that you are writing this for *you* and not as a document for your proposal. That comes later.

A. Find one or two examples of a literature review published in a referred journal. Most journals publish literature reviews, and the term *literature review* is often in the title. Some journals focus exclusively on literature reviews. For example, the Wiley-Blackwell publishing company (http://blackwell-compass .com) produces a series of peer-reviewed journals in history, sociology, geography and other disciplines where the articles are exclusively literature reviews. Examine the organization, content, and message presented in these articles.

B. Construct a thesis statement for the overall literature review. This is the main idea of the introductory paragraph. Your thesis statement (based on your focus earlier) should argue for a particular perspective on your subject, one you carry throughout your review. This could be a theoretical or conceptual framework. Some examples include the following:

The current trend in the sociology of family is to quantify fertility trends by economic and educational status.

The current trend in urban climatology is to use ASTER data to calculate the urban heat island.

The current trend in water resource conservation is to test educational outreach programs and their impact on water use.

C. Narrow the themes. There is no need to describe everything known about a particular topic (e.g., immigration, children's health), just the relevant issues. After reading your literature review, the reader should be able to identify the discourse in your research subject. What are the major themes or ideas surrounding the articles you have read? Do they use different methods? Do they find different solutions? Is there a trend or a big debate? As you read articles, you need to determine a particular focus (which becomes your structure).

D. Organize your writing into the following, obviously broad, sections, along with other sections that include your themes or organizing framework. A literature review needs to be structured. It needs to have (at the very least) the following:

    I. *An introduction.* The introduction needs to describe your main thesis, the motivation for the subsequent organization, and the structure of the rest of the document.

    II. *A main body.* The main body needs structure. The structure can be chronological, thematic, by a trend, or by methods. Remember, if you find each paragraph is a summary of an article, you do not have structure. In fact, you have a literature summary rather than a literature review. Don't just transpose your annotated bibliography to this section—it won't work.

    III. *Conclusions.* What have you learned from the literature? Where can the work go from here? Identify the holes that need to be researched.

    IV. *References cited.* A complete bibliographic reference is mandatory.

The number of references (e.g., books, chapters, journal articles) can vary dramatically depending on the subject area, the expectations of your advisor or committee, and the discipline's traditions. There is no right or wrong here. However, there should be at least 25 referred articles or books and 5,000 words (not including the references cited). As you write, be sure to put the ideas into your own words. Use quotes sparingly and watch how you paraphrase other work. Include your references at the end of the paper.

5. REVIEW AND REVISE

Two steps remain; both important but often easily dismissed.

A. Proofread your own work. Placing yourself in the frame of a "critical reader" often requires you to set it aside for a few days (a week is best). Afterward, read and evaluate it as if it is not your own work. Does the structure make sense? Are the ideas complete and connected? Revise accordingly. Use the writing toolbox in Chapter 5 to assist you.

B. Get external feedback. Ask one or more people to read and comment on your work. I recommend asking your advisor and one of your fellow graduate students. Give them at least a week to read and provide feedback. If they tell you a certain part doesn't make sense, you need to interpret that as an indication that you didn't express yourself well instead of responding with "Well, they just don't know enough about XYZ to understand my meaning." Remember, it is incumbent upon the author to make sure the readers—who are educated and intelligent—know enough about XYZ to understand the key message. And don't take their critiques personally; use them as feedback. It can be hard to see your document covered with comments. But take each one seriously.

Remaining Remarks

How long will the literature review take? This is not a weekend project. Remember that collecting and reading articles takes time. While online resources make collecting the material to read quite efficient, there is still effort (and time) required to keep what has been collected organized. (Those of us from the pre-Internet generation have memories of hours in the library, digging through journals, and photocopying article after article after article.) It also takes time to read articles and books. Skimming to "get the gist" is okay at the beginning, but eventually you have to take the plunge and read a paper from start to finish (or middle to end, beginning to middle). It is likely you will spend the better part of a day reading one (yes one) article. This is particularly true when the article is central to your work, when it is highly theoretical or abstract, or when there are a lot of mathematical equations. You need to spend the time to understand exactly what the author(s) did. Sometimes reading a single article requires you look at other articles to gain insight into the article of interest. Be prepared for that too. Furthermore, when you read an article, you need time to mentally synthesize what you are reading and weave it into the fabric of your previous knowledge. Other work, along with sleep and exercise, allows your brain to perform this important function.

Since I did not answer the earlier question on how long this will take, I will now. You should spend *at least* 4 or 5 solid weeks working on this first stage of the literature review for a first draft. This is a fast pace and includes at least 1 week for receiving feedback, which gives you less than 3 weeks for the reading and writing.

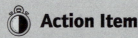

Action Item

In a sentence or two, describe the theoretical framework for your research. If this question challenges you, try it again after doing the following:

– Review the thesis statement of your literature review.
– Revisit the section on theoretical framework in this chapter.
– Reread a highly ranked article and decipher the theoretical framework the investigators used as a basis for problem solving.

Reminders

- Begin with the literature and then derive research questions.
- The literature review is not a summary of articles.
- Include both what was studied and what was found.
- Report on what is relevant to your research, not everything you know.
- Obtain and respond to feedback.

References

Kuhn, T. S. (1996). *The structure of scientific revolutions* (3rd ed.). Chicago: University of Chicago Press.

Punch, K. F. (2006). *Developing effective research proposals.* Thousand Oaks, CA: Sage.

8

The Academic Village

Introduction

The previous chapter addressed how to write a literature review. While knowledge of the literature and the players plays a pivotal role in your academic career, a nearby community is also involved deeply in your professional (and sometimes personal) development. This chapter provides guidelines on how to work effectively with your advisor, how to select the members of your graduate committee, and how to use faculty and others as you work to develop your research proposal and earn your degree. The guidelines provided here are aimed primarily at the traditional in-person graduate program. Students involved in a distance or online program will likely have different experiences. For example, face-to-face meetings may be conducted via Internet teleconferences.

The reasons for placing this chapter here—rather than at the beginning or end of the book—is because it is time to take a break from the depth of writing a proposal. Time helps to process the information gathered from reading the literature. It is also a good time to assess your topic and work by the people around you.

Advisor

During the graduate program, an important person is your academic advisor. Illustrating this, some academic fields document "academic genealogy" where advisor-student relationships are recorded in genetically based terminology (e.g., *academic grandfather*). When selecting an advisor, students become part of an academic family. There are academic genealogy reports in many fields, such as psychology, computer science, biology, and mathematics. These records illustrate how the schools of thought are passed from one academic generation to the next.

SELECTING AN ADVISOR

The obvious starting point in selecting an advisor is to identify faculty with similar research interests. In smaller programs, there may not be a choice; larger programs often provide several choices. Matching interests is a good start, but there are other considerations too, including an advisor's academic rank, his or her availability, and the personality match between you.

With more than one advisor candidate, start by knowing the person's academic position and university rank. The academic position refers to a tenured or tenure-track professor. In some institutions, this is a requirement. Potentially, the person also needs to be a member of the graduate or research faculty. Graduate faculty members are actively conducting research, and therefore the university grants permission to this group to supervise graduate students. Finally, identify the university rank—assistant, associate, or full professor. This identifies his or her level of experience as a professor.

There are tradeoffs with an advisor at each rank. An assistant professor has likely started his or her job within the last 6 years. This is good as the advisor relates closely to your experiences because he or she remembers the ins and outs of being a graduate student. His or her advising style is derived primarily from the advising style witnessed in pursuit of his or her own degree and from observing other faculty advise. Such an advisor's style, however, is probably more experimental. Additionally, standards are sometimes higher with an assistant professor. This is because the assistant professor may believe his or her reputation as an advisor, colleague, and professional are at stake. The assistant professor does not want to have his or her first student distribute a partially complete or poor-quality manuscript to the rest of the committee (i.e., peers and colleagues). That would be embarrassing and potentially damaging to his or her reputation. For you, this might involve more challenging hurdles (e.g., qualifying exams). The positive side? High standards mean your dissertation will rock!

Associate professors are typically more experienced than assistant professors in both research and teaching. Because of that, they have generally advised several undergraduate and graduate students. If you have selected an associate professor advisor, find out how many graduate committees (both as an advisor and a committee member) he or she has served on. Consider talking to current students to learn more about his or her advising style. Many consider the associate professor years as the mostly highly productive of a professor's career. The downside of this productivity is that he or she (who still lacks that final promotion to full professor) may believe there is something left to prove. The associate professor also lacks the seasoned experience of advising that many full professors have. He or she is still fine-tuning an advising style. The advantages though may outweigh these challenges. It is at this stage that the associate professor may make his or her most notable work. For a graduate student like you, this means you can latch on to this creative energy and produce an amazing dissertation.

A full professor likely has at least 10 years of experience in research, teaching, and—most importantly from your perspective—advising graduate students. The full professor is well known in the field. This is important because when you are in the job market, a full endorsement by him or her will open doors for you. Given the professor's own reputation, he or she is hopefully emotionally secure and will not be threatened by you, a talented, intelligent, and up-and-coming academic superstar. You will have the pleasure of a seasoned advisor because former students have taught him or her the best method for advising. He or she has read many theses and dissertations and knows how to provide concise and specific advice on how to move you through the program. In the end, you will have an impressive dissertation.

Experience clearly plays a role in how to pick an advisor. Other matters, which do not necessarily depend on rank, are the amount of time he or she has available to you, whether the person has other students that he or she is advising, and whether his or her advising style matches your needs. Ask a professor directly if he or she has time to advise you and how many other students he or she is advising. The professor may not have time because of administrative responsibilities or other commitments that require a significant number of meetings or travel. The number of students being advised can also play a role in the dynamics between you and your advisor. With only one or two students, you are like an only child and receive all the attention (which may be good) and expectations (also may be a good thing). With a large number, say nine or more, you become one of a pack. The upside is that you and your fellow studies can rely on each other, and you may move efficiently through the system with the pack. The time your advisor has for your work individually, however, may be smaller.

 Action Item

Regardless of whether you have an advisor, learn about the faculty in your unit. Go to the unit's website and read the biographies of the faculty. Note their academic rank and research interests. Meet with several whose interests overlap yours to discuss your academic trajectory (as you best see it now).

ADVISING STYLE

Advising style refers to the moment-to-moment interaction between student and advisor. This can include selecting classes, making sure university or unit deadlines are met, contacting committee members, and deciding the subject and content of the dissertation. Some professors are hands-off. They regard earning the degree as the student's responsibility. And ultimately, this is true. In contrast, other professors are similar to "helicopter parents" and participate in many aspects of the degree. Advising styles are a continuum, and this continuum can shift during the degree program and from student to student. Some specific questions you should ask yourself and then discuss with your advisor are the following: Who decides your research topic? How do you decide on the methods? When do you provide written work? When can you expect feedback? How often can you expect to have research meetings? Consider how these match your needs and expectations.

Critical from this list is having regular contact with your advisor to discuss your progress and plan. These meetings are essential for receiving feedback and efficiently progressing through the degree program. How often you meet depends both on you and your advisor. Simply put, there are regular meetings (daily or weekly) and irregular meetings. The tradeoffs for meeting frequency are summarized in Table 8.1.

You and your advisor may decide you want to have daily meetings (at least during the work week) at a specific time. This will mean regular feedback on the issues you are facing. You will share successes and disappointments immediately. You may also have very little to discuss since you just saw him or her the day before. Some meetings will be short and others long. Regardless, respect your advisor's time and he or she will also respect yours.

Regular meetings can be weekly, biweekly, or monthly and are ideally scheduled on the same day at the same time for a specified duration. The weekly interval is short enough to keep students from drifting and long enough to make progress toward the degree. Biweekly and monthly meetings mean that substantive progress has been made and the issues discussed are substantive. I suggest to my students that they provide me with written work for feedback. During the meeting, we can then discuss the details of how work is progressing.

An ad-hoc meeting schedule is often appropriate for both students and faculty. This style works because each meeting time is structured with specific topics and goals. These meetings may not deal with the frequent questions of the research but instead focus on major hurdles. Meeting times may be as far apart as several weeks or in some cases several months. The advantage for the student is that feedback is given when needed. The disadvantage occurs when a student needs help and waits too long to come see his or her advisor, believing the problem should be solved independently.

Table 8.1 Pros and cons of meeting styles between the student and advisor.

Meeting Frequency	Advantages	Disadvantages
Daily	It offers frequent opportunity to interact. Student and/or faculty may feel their time is being intruded upon.	Meetings may be too short to accomplish enough.
Weekly (biweekly)	Enough time lapses between meetings that tasks can be accomplished. It keeps student accountable on a short time frame.	You may have questions or issues that need to be addressed in between meetings. Little work may have been accomplished for real feedback to occur.
Monthly	Meeting content is substantive.	It may not be often enough to get feedback. Major issues may arise between meetings.
Ad hoc	You see your advisor when you need him or her. You know what needs to be covered.	He or she may not be available as soon as you want. Students may need meetings and not set them because they don't realize the benefit.

Regardless of the meeting frequency, the meeting agenda remains the student's responsibility. That is, you should plan an agenda that includes recent progress, a future plan, and specific questions. A sample agenda is shown in Figure 8.1. An agenda means time with your advisor will be effective and efficient, which means you will be that much closer to earning your degree.

Figure 8.1 Sample meeting agenda by a PhD candidate.

Mar 29, 2011

- Research Topic 2: Green Index Paper
  - I couldn't complete yet. I have some questions for the revision.
  - I have attached your revision comments for the discussion.

(Continued)

Figure 8.1   (Continued)

- Schedule for Next Steps

  o Research Topic 2: Green Index Paper > April 5
  o Research Topic 1: Fuzzy Open Space Mapping > April 19
  o Research Topic 3: Economic Part Introduction and Literature Review > April 26
  o Research Topic 3: Economic Part Data Preparation and Analysis > May 3
  o Research Topic 3: Data Preparation and Analysis > May 10

- Meeting with Dr Victor Mesev
- Hourly Work

 Action Item

Schedule a meeting with your advisor. Bring an agenda to the meeting that includes what you have accomplished and your plans. Include in your plan a point to discuss your advisor's view of your research trajectory and expectations of your proposal-writing timetable.

MENTOR VERSUS FRIEND

Your advisor can be both your mentor and friend. A mentor is a person who imparts knowledge, influences thinking, and guides careers. A friend is a person who cares about you as an individual and demonstrates that affection over time with encouragement and support. Your advisor can (and in my opinion should) be both your mentor and your friend.

Activities you should expect from your advisor as a mentor include guidance on the courses you take, who else serves on your committee, your research proposal, and ultimately your dissertation. For some graduate students, this is sufficient and may be all you can receive from your advisor. Other students depend on more than this, and this is when an advisor becomes a mentor. A mentor's role involves influencing the way you think by sharing experiences with you about when he or she completed his or her own PhD, such as how to schedule your day to be more efficient. A mentor can also guide your career by introducing you to key researchers in your field or by encouraging you to introduce yourself to them.

One of the characteristics of a good advisor is someone who pushes you outside your comfort zone. For example, I attended my first academic meeting with my advisor. At the meeting, there was an esteemed researcher whose work I followed. In the past, my advisor had introduced me to a few of his colleagues and I knew that he and this esteemed researcher knew one another. I wanted to meet him, and I asked my advisor to introduce me to him. He said no! I couldn't believe it. He said, "You need to go up to him and introduce yourself." After settling down from the shock and working up the nerve, I finally went up to the man and introduced myself. This was an important lesson about how to network at professional meetings, but it taught me to move outside my comfort zone and be a little more outgoing and assertive than I normally feel. He became an important mentor during my career, and I now regard him as a good friend.

In an interesting turn of events, in 2011, I attended an invitation-only reception at an annual professional meeting accompanied by the esteemed researcher—now friend—I introduced myself to two decades earlier. I came to the reception unprepared for the style, which was formal business attire (I should have known better . . . really). I was wearing running shoes, blue jeans, and a fleece jacket, plus I was carrying a Starbucks souvenir bag. Intimidated by the room of people I thought I did not know, I said to my friend, "This is not the place for me. I need to leave." He turned to me and said something to the effect of, "No, these are the movers and shakers of our field. You need to stay and interact with these people." He (wearing a jacket and tie incidentally) introduced me to a small group, but soon after I was off on my own. I introduced myself to people I did not know and I found there were also people I knew. While I still struggled with how to carry my Starbucks bag, I left the reception feeling pleased with the professional inter-actions that took place but also reflecting on the push my advisor gave me to meet the esteemed colleague decades earlier. Later, I also purchased a nice professional-looking carrying case for my laptop to replace the tattered back-pack I had carried to the conference.

As the time spent with your advisor grows, you may find that in addition to mutual work interests, you have personal interests too. My PhD advisor and I have had many shopping excursions together. I know several graduate stu-dents who play sports or share other mutual interests with their advisor. There are times however when your advisor needs to be just your mentor and not your friend. There can be difficult periods when you are working on your degree: developing your research proposal, taking comprehensive exams, or later in the process when finishing your dissertation. During these difficult periods, it may seem as if your advisor is no longer your friend because the feedback you are getting is harsh and seems no longer supportive. During these times a good advisor will put aside (temporarily) the friend hat and firmly place the mentor hat on his or her head. Although a good friend will also give you honest feedback even if it is not what you want to hear. Your advisor knows that the best path for you to finish your degree may be the hardest, and he or she will put you down that path. It is hard and frustrating for both because you may fear your friendship is being destroyed. In some cases, that may happen. In other cases, it will not. Whether the friendship stays intact or not depends mostly on how the graduate student views this transition. If the graduate student can reflect and recognize that the difficult periods were really in their best interest and the best path to completion, then the friendship will survive.

YOUR ADVISOR'S ROLE

As you meet with your advisor over the duration of your graduate career, you may find you talk about a variety of topics beyond the dissertation. Maybe you have favorite books in common or share restaurant choices. Conversations may even become more personal too, such as discussing relationship or marital issues. Through this process, you may come to view your advisor as a confidant. In the long run, the two of you may become close personal friends.

In the meantime, however, the primary role of your advisor is to provide you with guidance on earning your degree. Early on this may involve helping you decide the best courses to take. He or she may suggest faculty who become part of your committee. He or she will talk with you about the requirements associated with comprehensive or qualifying exams and will help you with your proposal. This involves helping you narrow your topic to something meaningful and worthwhile. It also involves helping you identify the appropriate methods and write in the appropriate style. Advisors also help determine whether the project is doable in the allotted time and with the allotted resources. He or she provides feedback as you do the research. The advisor is also part of assessing your work when it is complete; he or she tells you when it is ready to share with your committee or submit for publication. Hopefully he or she will take you out for lunch from time to time.

During lunch, you may talk more about research. The conversation also may drift into learning more about one another as people. In situations like this, find out more about your advisor when he or she was in graduate school. In other words, learn about your academic genealogy. Through the process, you may learn why he or she attended a particular school. You may find too that lunch conversations as well as professional traveling are opportunities to become friends as well as strengthen the student-advisor relationship. Some students shy away from this, but my view is if you get along and enjoy your advisor's company, there is nothing wrong with it. There are boundaries though that need to be clearly marked and followed.

One vague boundary you should observe is depending on your advisor for emotional guidance. Table 8.2 identifies the difference between what typically is and is not your advisor's responsibility. While advisors often have "life skill" suggestions, they should not be put in the position of therapist or psychologist. It is also up to the advisor to know these boundaries too. Understandably, students become distressed over many issues such as test scores, final grades, and rejected manuscripts. There is a boundary, however, between listening to a distressed student about a course and helping a student with mental health problems. Your advisor is not likely trained as a therapist, psychologist, or psychiatrist and is not responsible for your mental health. Fortunately, universities have staff psychologists or psychiatrists for students. There is an understanding that earning a degree (either undergraduate or graduate) is stressful and people need help. Help is a private

Table 8.2   Advisor responsibilities.

Advisor's Responsibility	Not Advisor's Responsibility
Course suggestions	Making sure you have the required courses completed
Suggesting possible committee members	The number of credit hours you need
Discussing research topics	Knowing university deadlines for milestone completion
Reviewing written material (e.g., proposal, dissertation)	Knowing the funding opportunities available to you (scholarships, fellowships, assistantships)
Providing professional guidance on career options	Staying in touch with your committee with progress
Writing recommendation letters for fellowships, grant applications, jobs	Scheduling meetings and exams with your committee
Watching your mental health	Fixing your mental health

matter—no one needs to know you are going. Professionals can help with depression, anxiety, or thoughts of suicide. If your mental health is preventing you from moving forward with your degree, seek the help you need. It will make a difference.

The one obvious hard boundary is that the relationship with your advisor should not become intimate. Universities have clear rules on this covering both consensual and nonconsensual relationships. While a consensual relationship may seem okay, the power roles become unbalanced. The person who makes professional decisions about progress through the program may become biased. A nonconsensual relationship is sexual harassment. This is any unwelcome sexual advance, used for intimidation. If you (or a fellow graduate student) have questions about this or encounter problems, seek professional university help. All universities have resources that provide anonymous guidance on how to handle unwelcome advances.

CHANGING YOUR ADVISOR

There are cases where you and the advisor you selected are a poor match. The reasons vary but could be based on mismatched research interests, methodological differences, not converging on a dissertation topic, advising style, or strictly personality conflicts. Hopefully this mismatch is identified early in the graduate program and you can switch before either of you becomes too invested. But because of the strong connection between advisors and students, it can be an awkward and difficult task to approach the "divorce." My recommendation is to be honest and direct without being accusing or negative. The advisor probably has the same sense that your relationship is not working, and he or she probably will not be surprised by the conversation. Make the conversation face to face instead of through e-mail. The poorest way to handle this situation is to "slink away" to another advisor without letting your current advisor know. He or she will eventually find out (e.g., the public announcement of your dissertation defense at the very latest) and that reflects poorly on you.

GET FEEDBACK

The most important thing you need from your advisor is feedback. You will progress much faster when you receive feedback sooner rather than later. While this starts when you are discussing which courses to take and can be managed by an oral conversation, most of the feedback you need should be in written form. This means you need to provide something in writing too. Remember that in the end, your dissertation will be a written document so you need to start writing early and receive feedback as soon as possible. As an advisor, I find it frustrating to have an oral conversation about written work such as methods or results. The picture is unclear and the structure of the document is difficult to follow. Instead, provide your advisor with written materials even when they are just ideas. Each time you submit something to your advisor, make it your best effort even when incomplete. While you will still receive critical comments, you know you did your best.

Committee

There are three reasons to have a research committee (above and beyond the fact that most institutions require it). The first is that people bring different knowledge and skills to the table. Even two people who generally specialize in the same topic will approach it differently. One may be more theoretically based; the other may have a policy perspective. The second is that these different knowledge bases result in different perspectives. Different perspectives result in broader and deeper comprehension of your problem and the solutions you find. Third, when viewed from more than one perspective, research proposals and results are better validated. If one person says, "This is great stuff" and the remaining think, "There is no merit here," then it is back to the drawing board. In the end, when the committee is satisfied, everyone (you, your advisor, committee members, your academic unit, and the university) is more confident in placing the official stamp of approval on your final dissertation. Evaluation from multiple people is not limited to dissertations; it is also why two or more people review research grants and referred journal papers before a decision is made.

Committee members play a significant role from the beginning of the degree. Initially, you will likely meet prospective committee members in the courses you take. In fact, I once had a rule that anyone who wanted me to serve on his or her committee needed to take at least one of my courses. I figured that if my subject area (embedded of course in the courses I taught) matched their interests, then they should be taking my courses. That turned out to be impractical for several reasons, but it remains a reasonable starting point for students. Later, committee members typically serve on qualifying or candidacy exams, on proposal and dissertation defenses, and eventually as reference letter writers.

The success of this whole process of course rests on selecting the right people with the right skills to serve the student. The obvious criterion is people who complement the research interests and skills of your advisor with research interests and skills you need to complete your dissertation. One starting point is to consider former instructors as candidates. Other candidates are faculty in your academic unit or from other academic units. I find that student success increases with highly diverse committees. This improves breadth of knowledge areas, depth from different perspectives, and stronger validation.

Above and beyond the research interests of committee members, I value diversity in student committees. Diversity comes from faculty from different academic subjects, as mentioned, as well as academic rank. For example, students should pick committee members who recently earned their PhD. There is considerable value in including someone who has just experienced the process—he or she remembers the process well. Furthermore, the experience of being on a PhD committee helps that person build his or her own experience. These people are often newly appointed assistant professors or postdoctoral research faculty.

Finally, avoid having too many people on your committee. You may be fortunate to attend a university with numerous faculty who are excellent scholars, are interested in your research, are available, and get along well. My recommendation is to start with the minimum number required by the university and add someone only if necessary. One simple disadvantage of too many is scheduling the in-person meetings and exams.

If the occasion occurs (and it sometimes does) where you need to remove a committee member, inform that person as soon as possible. The best is to meet with him or her in person and say you have decided to make a change in your committee. There is no need to go into great detail describing the reason. Regardless, say it with respect.

After selecting candidate committee members, consider these questions:

Do they seem to be interested in your research? Faculty who have done work in a subject area may or may not still be interested in that topic. It is important to ask if they are willing to serve on your committee *after* they have had the chance to talk to you or read about your area of interest.

Are they available to meet with you? On the one hand, it is an honor to have a prestigious scientist serve on your committee. On the other hand, it is also part of their job description to mentor students. It is pretty easy to tell if professors have time to meet with students. When you do meet, see if they talk to you or check their e-mail and act distracted. Talk with other more senior students about the availability of different professors.

Do members of the committee get along well? You might not know the answer to this question, but your advisor or students further along in the program may have some insights. There can be strong opinions among faculty and occasionally a bit less than the utmost respect for one another. (To say it plainly, sometimes faculty don't get along.) In many cases, faculty will look past these differences in the interest of serving students, but that may not always be the case. If you know prospective committee members are actively collaborating, then you probably do not need to worry about it. In other cases, it is worthwhile to ask about the relationships between prospective committee members.

Do you like the person? This may or may not be relevant to everyone, but for me it was important. I suggest it to my students too because you need to spend time with your committee. If the person is disagreeable to you on any level, it is not a good match.

Other Faculty

Whether you take a class from a professor or simply exchange greetings in the hallway, it is important to know a little bit about each of the faculty in your unit. In one of the early semesters of your degree, take time to spend 5 minutes with each faculty member (during office hours of course) to say hello, ask about his or her research, and share your interests. You never know when that 5-minute interaction will pay off.

There are also occasions when engagement with another faculty member will be closer than simply hallway greetings. Professors can provide ad-hoc advice on numerous subjects. There may be a professor who earned his or her PhD at a university where you have a job interview. You may learn more inside information by speaking with him or her about former colleagues. Obtaining advice on various topics with noncommittee faculty is common but should not be abused either. If the person is a pseudo–committee member, he or she is doing the work and not receiving the appropriate credit. Remember, when a student earns a degree, the advisor and committee members receive recognition for this accomplishment too. In other words, avoid taking advantage of someone's time without giving the person due credit.

Part of the reason your interaction with other professors is important is because they are your colleagues. Some faculty view graduate students as students and others label them as "junior colleagues." While there is still a differentiation between students and faculty in terms of experience (and salary!), the same can be said about this differentiation between assistant professors and full professors. The term *colleague* is more appropriate because students will, in a short amount of time, become just colleagues, not "junior" colleagues. There is no reason to make the "junior" distinction in graduate school. The term *colleague* suggests respect between both parties.

Graduate Students

Graduate students take the same classes as you, work late into the night with you, socialize with you, share hotel rooms with you at academic conferences, compete against you for grants and jobs, and become lifelong friends. It is important to be engaged as much as possible with fellow graduate students because more than anyone, they support you and they need your support. Undergraduate students looking at prospective graduate programs need to examine the cohesiveness of the graduate students as an indicator of the program's quality. It tells all. The remainder of this section discusses how to interact with fellow graduate students.

DISSERTATION SUPPORT GROUP (DSG)

A dissertation support group, or DSG, is a small group of students who meet regularly to provide academic and personal support while in the throes of earning a degree. You can successfully earn a PhD without a DSG. However, a DSG provides support, reminders, and peer pressure on many levels. Here are some ways a DSG helps.

Prioritizing

A DSG can help you prioritize day-to-day or week-to-week activities. Deciding what to do next can sometimes seem daunting. Each of us has a never-ending list of things to do. Some of these are low-hanging fruit—they do not seem to take much time or they seem (at the moment) to be the most important. Often, we neglect that mountainous activity that really should be at the top of the list. If you have "write dissertation proposal" on your to-do list, it will feel imposing and impossible to do. Breaking down that activity into manageable tasks helps prioritize it. Bolker's (1998) *Writing Your Dissertation in Fifteen Minutes a Day* describes how to break through writer's block, which is often the source of poor prioritization. Remind yourself (or get those reminders with a DSG) that spending 3 hours to read thoroughly a really good article is part of "write dissertation proposal" just like spending 3 hours to write a single paragraph.

Time Management

The twin to prioritizing is time management. A DSG talks about day-to-day planning. It is one thing to set a goal for a week; it is another to enable it to work each day. The best advice of course is to work each and every day. The "destroyer" is to set aside a single day to "really get some work done." Yes, some days you work hour after hour; some days less. But each day requires attention. The "something every day" plan also works for diet, exercise, sleep, piano practice, and the other essentials of life.

Feedback

Everyone needs someone else to read his or her work and provide substantive feedback. It is part of the process. It is helpful to run work past a DSG before sharing it with your advisor. It is also part of the responsibility of academics to read other people's work and provide feedback. Reading the work of DSG buddies provides you with that experience.

Peer Pressure

You appear at the weekly meeting with less done than you expected. A DSG buddy shares her report and has really made progress. Gulp. It is your turn. What happened? You think, if they can do it, so can I. Peer pressure can motivate you to stay on top of your game.

Problem Solving

Sometimes you just need someone to listen to your problem. Heck, that is why there are counselors and therapists. The problems a DSG can solve include how to find an obscure reference, how to respond to reviewer comments, specifics questions on how to operate a computer program, and how to deal with competition among fellow graduate students. Sometimes responses are direct feedback ("go to the reference librarian (duh)") and other times there is little direct response but just someone listening. More often than not, just thinking out loud is sufficient to resolve issues.

Personality Conflicts

It is inevitable that learning and working in an environment with intelligent, motivated, and hardworking individuals will lead to conflict. Most often conflicts are between advisor and advisee. Other conflicts may be between you and your committee members, other graduate students, or family and friends. There is no one better to support you through this than your DSG. Worst case, however, is when the conflict is within the DSG. My advice? Get over it.

Lifelong Friendship

A DSG may or may not result in lifelong friendships, but it can.

SOME GUIDING PRINCIPLES

The following list reflects guidelines on how to form and conduct a DSG so you benefit the most from the experience.

1. Start the group during the first or second year of the program.

Groups can form at any stage and are vitally important from proposal writing to degree completion. However, I do recommend you form your group so you are together for at least a year if not more. That way you have time to earn the trust and gain the support from each other.

2. Pick a small committed group.

The most successful DSGs have three or four committed members at roughly the same stage of earning their degree. There is generally a lot of interest in forming a DSG because it sounds like such a great idea (which it is!). You may find that 10 or more people want to be included. The first meeting will be a hit. Then when it comes to meeting again and regularly, only two or so actually show up (and it won't always be the same two or so). This is frustrating and not supportive. They have excuses—a paper due, grading. The point of the DSG however is to be supportive so that deadlines like these are not looming beacons of stress.

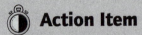

Action Item

Pick two or three people who work well together. Suggest to others if interested that they should form their own groups.

3. Consider the dynamics.

It is slightly better if each person in a DSG has a different primary advisor. This is so you can hear from a DSG how other advisors suggest situations are handled. So in an indirect way you have another advisor. Pick people knowledgeable enough about your subject matter. This is good because you read and provide feedback on writing or ideas through a knowledgeable yet general lens. Other DSGs have been successful with a mixture of disciplines too. This too is a good model in the new trans-, cross-, multidisciplinary world of academia.

4. Have a regular meeting time.

During the peak of your work (dissertation writing primarily), meet weekly for about an hour. Our group had a set time and place and there was no need to confirm. If memory serves, we never had a no-show. The consistency of meeting regularly helped me maintain a writing pace that helped me earn my degree.

5. Meet away from the office.

When the weather is nice, meet at a park. In bad weather, meet at a local coffee shop. Enjoy the secluded, away-from-the-office experience of the meetings. The nonoffice settings provide you with neutrality to pull you away from strictly shop talk, diversity to open up minds to new ideas, and privacy needed to vent about frustrations.

6. Have an agenda.

One way to operationalize the meeting is to have each person bring a progress report and plan for the next week. Take turns sharing your plan and progress with each other and provide feedback. Feedback could mean prioritizing activities, peer pressure (e.g., "Why didn't get you get such-and-such done?"), or direct feedback on writing. Sometimes include in your plan to share writing with the group, which can be e-mailed in advance. After the plan and progress round-robin, you can open the meeting up for general discussion (e.g., venting).

GOING FORWARD

After reading several books (such as those listed in the references) on earning a PhD and academic writing, I realized writing support groups are common advice. The success of this model was reaffirmed in Roberts (2010) and Bolker (1998) on dissertation support groups and Silva (2007) on academic writing support. Silva (2007) describes a writing support group for academics similar to a DSG that he calls Agraphia. It goes without saying that I (and others) highly recommend it.

Family and Friends

Many people move to a new city or even a different country to attend graduate school. Typically, this means living far away from immediate family and past friends. This is a difficult transition, particularly for someone who completed a bachelor's degree closer to home. Foreign students are particularly susceptible to homesickness and the challenges of a different culture and perhaps even a new language. It is therefore critical to stay in touch with family and friends as much as possible but also forge ahead and make new friends.

For those fortunate enough to live with or near family, the same rules apply—perhaps even more so. Organize the day's activities to include family time because in your acknowledgments, you will likely describe how important family support was in finishing your degree.

Academic friends are important, but so are nonacademic friends. Close nonacademic friends of mine include a stay-at-home mom, a realtor, a project consultant, a hospital computer administrator, an occupational therapist, and a self-employed landscape architect. You can meet such friends through other interests such as hiking, bicycling, Girl Scouts, children (if you have them), and participating in community activities. These connections bring diversity to your life by reminding you that other professions can be stressful too and that letting go sometimes is important. In your constant quest for knowledge, you can learn a tremendous amount from these friends too. You can share books and talk about the things you read. But beyond these direct differences, some of these friends approach problems differently from the academic community. This different way of looking at the world can help you have a broader outlook, serving you well in your own profession.

As I state in later chapters, it is important to make proposal writing specifically (and graduate school and life as an academic as a whole) a way of life and not a race to a single objective. Sometimes academics say they do not have time for extra friends; they are just too busy. I argue, however, that friends and family maintain physical and emotional health. Physical health involves eating right and exercising. You need to make time for these—why not do them with your friends? These activities are important too for emotional health. For one thing, good food and exercise are essential for optimal brain functioning. But more than that, eating and exercising provide an opportunity to talk, which is great stress relief (even guys less prone to venting benefit emotionally from exercising with friends).

Evaluating and taking care of emotional health is trickier than physical health. A partial explanation is because it is difficult to determine when emotional problems are within the normal ebb and flow of life and when professional help is needed beyond what family and friends can offer. A second explanation is because there is a stigma with having mental health problems. Most campuses offer *confidential* student mental health services. Anyone feeling overwhelmed, anxious, depressed, or suicidal must seek out these resources. Use these services if you need them—your brain will thank you.

Reminders

- Advisors are the foundation of the research trajectory.
- Take charge of meetings with your advisor.
- Advisors are mentors but can be friends too.
- Respect the time and effort of your committee and other faculty.
- A DSG is part of your academic training by receiving and providing feedback.
- Be committed to your DSG; don't bail on meetings or responsibilities.

References

Bolker, J. (1998). *Writing your dissertation in fifteen minutes a day: A guide to starting, revising, and finishing your doctoral thesis*. New York: Owl Books.

Roberts, C. M. (2010). *The dissertation journey: A practical and comprehensive guide to planning, writing, and defending your dissertation* (2nd ed.). Thousand Oaks, CA: Sage.

Silvia, P. (2007). *How to write a lot: A practical guide to productive academic writing*. Washington, DC: American Psychological Association.

Acknowledgements: Duane Marble, Donna Peuquet, Robin Leichenko, Karen Arabas, and Karen O'Brien.

9

Conceptualizing a Research Idea

Introduction

The literature review written from Chapter 7 is your vision of the existing research structure and illustrates your view of the linkages between the ideas of previous work in your area of specialization. What emerged was a description of what has been studied, what is known about those topics, and the questions that remain unanswered. The next goal is to decide which of the unanswered or unsolved problems interest you and which can be turned into specific research questions or a problem statement for your own research proposal. In other words, you need to figure out what you are going to do.

Many guidelines on how to write a dissertation or thesis proposal make one simple assumption: that you know what you want to research and all you need to learn is how to write it up. But as Kamler and Thomson (2006) emphasize, writing is part of the research process (as is presenting, reviewing, and revising), and many students have not yet decided on a specific research topic. In line with Kamler and Thomson (2006), writing is part of figuring out what you want to do. The writing process is not simply something done at the end to explain what has been done. Writing is a tool to help decide what to do as well as how to do it. That is why writing activities persist throughout this book. This chapter is not an exception.

The research proposal identifies specific unknowns and unsolved problems with a certain level of specificity, but that step is saved for Chapter 10. Instead, this chapter helps you decide on and articulate a generalized research concept. You will be deciding on a general problem or abstract idea that you later turn into something more specific. The idea of a research concept is positioned higher on the spiral, implying that the content is more specific than the focused literature review and more general than the specific problem (see Figure 9.1).

Figure 9.1 A general research concept is more specific than the focused literature review and more general than the specific problem statement.

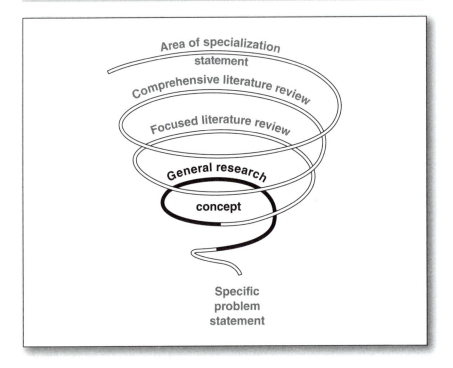

Integration Between the AOS and the Literature Review

The document you write for this chapter is positioned intellectually at the intersection between the area of specialization (AOS) statement and the literature review. It states that within the work everyone else has done, here sits a new problem area that needs to be solved. It aims to answer three basic questions: what, how, and why.

The process begins with *what* and could include one or more of the following questions:

What else can we know about something?

What can we do better?

What is a more complete explanation of something?

And deals with *how*:

> How has this problem been addressed by others?
>
> How will I do this differently?

And leads to *why*:

> Why do we want to know more about this?
>
> Why do we need to do it better?
>
> Why don't we understand this part?

The answers to these three questions form the basis for the generalized research concept.

Pathways to the Research Concept

There are three pathways to the research concept: from the top down, from the bottom up, and the random walk. All involve active reading and writing. The difference between them is how you move between the literature and the research question. It begins with the idea of a quest, or a journey with a particular goal. The goal here is a concept—an idea you want to develop into a research proposal. Arriving at that goal requires a journey into the unknown where unexpected challenges, opportunities, and lessons appear along the way. Here I describe how you might journey through the experience of discovering the research path.

TOP DOWN

Top down is often considered the ideal way to approach a research project. Most books and courses assume this path. This top-down approach to developing a research question moves from the top of the spiral (topical interest) toward the tip (a specific question). The path looks a little like this:

1. You are enrolled in a graduate program at a reputable university and your graduate mentor (advisor) is well known and respected in the subfield you wish to study.

2. You take seminars and coursework at the university. A paper you write for one course interests you and so you read further into a particular topic.

3. You read more about this particular topic and learn that little is known about a particular aspect of it. You discuss this topic with your advisor.

4. This unknown aspect becomes the basis for your research proposal. You decide on research questions and methods to solve questions and better understand this unknown part.

The advantages of this approach are that the theoretical framework is well known and established and the question you eventually pose fills a gap in the knowledge. The disadvantage is that it is often inefficient. It requires you to read extensively within and outside your area of interest. While your advisor may be able to steer you in a certain direction, the understanding of the theoretical framework and the unknown knowledge needs to be your own discovery. These steps however are idealized and do no incorporate sufficiently the opportunity and the need to explore and discover unknown pathways. The quest leads to the search for the unknown knowledge gap. The journey involves reading new literature and discovering for yourself what you do and do not know.

BOTTOM UP

Bottom up starts with a research question or a specific problem to solve. From there you approach the literature to discover how your question fits into the existing knowledge. The path looks something like this:

1. You enroll in a specific graduate program at a reputable university to work with a specific advisor on a topic that interests you.

2. You approach your PhD advisor for approval on an idea of a question or problem to solve. He or she asks you how this question fills a hole in the literature.

3. Knowing the subject matter, you attack the literature with a focused mission to see related topics. You verify that the problem remains unsolved.

4. You formulate a theoretical framework for your problem and demonstrate that your question fills gaps in the knowledge.

The advantages of the bottom-up approach are that the literature to read is focused and the question is already in place. These are also disadvantages because a narrow literature search may limit how the theoretical framework is structured, and the question may already be answered. Limiting the theoretical framework may mean too that the solution you seek is also narrow. If a question is developed before the necessary knowledge exists, it may be naïve because the issue has been thoroughly investigated before. There is of course the opportunity to fix these problems, but this pathway is the random walk. The quest here is for the theoretical framework that forms the structure for your research question. The journey involves learning what else has been investigated in that area and how it relates to what you want to solve.

RANDOM WALK

The random walk is a hybrid between the top-down and bottom-up approaches. The hybrid component involves iteratively moving between comprehending the literature and fine-tuning your research question. The random walk could start at any point along the spiral. The path looks something like this:

1. You enroll in a reputable graduate program; soon you meet an advisor whose subject matter interests you.

2. Because of readings or a conversation with someone, you or your advisor suggest a question or topic for you to address.

3. With that question or topic, you approach the literature. At this point, you are either refining the question or better formulating the theoretical framework.

4. Steps 2 and 3 are repeated until the question and the theoretical framework are in place.

The advantage of this approach is the process unfolds and allows for adjustments as new ideas and information become clear. The disadvantage is that arriving at the destination could take more time than a more direct approach. The reality is that most students (and many investigators) take the random-walk approach because as more is understood about the literature, the research question evolves. As the research question evolves, new aspects of the literature need to be understood. It is not an indication of poor (or random) science but rather an exercise in digging deeper and improved understanding.

ALTERNATE PATHWAYS

Research ideas do come from the literature, but they also come from other sources as well. They come from conversations with other people, material in coursework, and a whole suite of experiences that are difficult to articulate. Graduate students often turn to their advisor for recommendations. Students may have interest in a topic and recognize gaps in the knowledge but are unclear about a suitable way to approach the gaps as a research proposal. Students see the top or point of the spiral but are less clear about the content within the central rings. Seasoned investigators also turn to colleagues and experts for advice and ideas on how to proceed. Frequent collaborative interaction helps formulate interesting and innovative generalized research concepts and specific goals.

⏱ Action Item

Supporting the quest means stepping away from the path to find new information. In the next 2 or 3 weeks, attend a colloquium or dissertation defense in a field unrelated to your own. Learn about the new topic and the process. Engage by asking a question.

Set up a short-term reading group. Gather four to six graduate students (and professors if you can talk them into it) to have a miniseminar series. Have each person take a turn selecting a reading and meet a week later to discuss the selected papers.

Take some time to explore the content and scope of previously written dissertations. Most units retain hard copies of past dissertations and theses in in-unit libraries. The university library also has copies of all university dissertations and theses.

Application, Method, Theory

At this point in the activities toward a generalized research concept, the literature is a resource for new ideas. This step involves organizing existing research into three categories: application, method, and theory. *Application* refers to a project that uses existing theories and methods to solve a specific problem in a specific domain. A novel and doable project is to duplicate the research in a new setting—for example, a study group in a different geographic area. *Method* refers to a project that develops and tests new methods (e.g., data or analytical tools) for solving problems. A novel and doable project in this category involves modifying or creating a new tool that solves the same type of problem but in a new and "better" way. Finally, *theory* refers to a project that challenges existing theories by modifying or creating a new theory that explains a phenomenon in a way previous theories failed to do. Your own research question will eventually fit into one of these three categories.

In application, the question is whether the same principles hold by replicating an existing study in a different geographic area or with a different focus group. In some application methods investigators use a new dataset, alternative variables, or a different model to try to explain something better. Application is considered "low-hanging fruit." In other words, it is an easy problem to identify and the solutions are readily seen. For example, you may read about a paper that models air quality using an urban circulation model in Sydney. You can replicate this study by using the same methods but for data in Tampa. Depending on the similarities of the studies, this research is sometimes difficult to publish. This is true especially if the results are the same as the other study. The novelty of the work—how it has contributed to the literature—is harder to sell to editors of highly ranked journals. When categorizing research into application, the assumption is to solve a well-known problem with similar data but in a different contextual focus area (e.g., new focus group or new geographical area) that distinguishes it from prior research.

Methods are the building blocks for new research. It is the approach taken to solve a particular problem. Researchers are always on the lookout for new methods to solve their problems, and it is up to methods-based research to create the new approaches. The primary objective is to create something new and demonstrate that it works better than existing approaches. Developing a new approach may involve tweaking or adapting existing methods, or it could be something completely new. Demonstrating it is better than existing approaches requires that *better* is defined in a meaningful and testable way. When looking at other research to place in this category, you need to decide if it presents a new method and has been tested.

Theory is the foundation for new research. It provides the basis for how people think about and understand how something works. Often though, existing theories are imperfect. There are situations in which a theory is not effective or does not explain enough of a phenomenon. This motivates new research into adapting theories or creating new theories to explain something better. The research question becomes whether an alternative theory explains a phenomenon better. Typically a new theory does not emerge from nowhere. It is an idea generated from known knowledge and experience with existing theories. The theories with the largest incremental change are often those derived because ideas from one topic or field are integrated into a different one. The old ideas from one topic become transformative ideas in another field.

⏱ Action Item

Write a one-sentence description on the problem you want to solve by using the concepts of application, method, or theory. For example, your sentence could begin in one of the following ways:

By using the _____ theory and _____ methods, my goal is to better understand how _____. (Application)

The goal of the project is to create a new method to better _____. (Method)

The _____ theory to describe _____ is ineffective at explaining how _____ operates. My goal is to develop a new theory. (Theory)

An Example

As previously described, the pathway to a specific research question and subsequently a proposal can vary. As an example, I describe a specific path on how a research question to create a new method and the associated theoretical framework were formed. Presently, I am working on a research project designing decision support software (tools) that models the spatial interaction of nitrogen in New England watersheds. Realistically, this is a bottom-up approach because I started by developing the tool. Ultimately, my goal is to demonstrate that my tool solves problems in ways other software does not, so I need to understand what other software does to effectively make a comparison. To arrive at this goal, I need to know how my software *is* actually different and solves problems "better" than existing software. This requires knowledge of the domain—the literature on the subject. I need to know what is known about nitrogen in the environment and how other models have dealt with it. The big categories in the nitrogen literature are the following:

> *Nitrogen in the environment.* Historically nitrogen (N) was a limited element because it did not occur in the right form for plants to use; this has changed (mostly) because of the addition of anthropogenic sources (agricultural runoff and nonsewered residential).

> *The chemical interaction in the environment.* How and why it goes from N to a nitrogen gas (N_2).

> *Nitrogen sources.* Quantifying the naturally occurring and anthropogenic sources (e.g., residential and agriculture).

> *Nitrogen sinks.* Rivers, ponds, and streams remove excess nitrogen and turn it to nitrogen gas.

> *Nitrogen impacts.* Environmental: when in estuaries, eutrophication resulting in fish deaths; economic impacts to fishing industry.

> *Nitrogen modeling and software.* Some spatial, many focusing mostly on N sources.

> *Nitrogen policy.* How best management practices (BMP) can change nitrogen delivery.

The literature on nitrogen is vast (e.g., the keyword *nitrogen* in Web of Science retrieved 389,572 records on July 23, 2012). I used the processes described in Chapter 5 (Effective Reading) and Chapter 7 (Literature Review) to narrow the literature and focus on what is relevant to my interests. Since my interests are in spatial analysis and geospatial modeling, I added keywords such as *spatial* to the search and found articles within four of the previous broad categories of nitrogen research. My generalized research concept therefore is spatial modeling of nitrogen sources and sinks in the environment. In other words, in some cases, your generalized research interest may not fit within a single topic but be cross-cutting, as this example demonstrates.

🕐 To Do List

Like in the nitrogen project example, create a list of the research areas that cover the topic or problem that interests you. The goal with this activity is to remain somewhat broad but be more specific than you were in the area of specialization. Answer these questions to better understand how they form a theoretical framework.

1. What methods do the papers use? In the nitrogen example, I divided the literature into the methods that use spatial modeling and those that do not. While I keep the nonspatial modeling articles on hand to integrate elsewhere, the spatial modeling articles become my focus.

   Are you interested in developing a new method to study a problem?

2. What geographic study area is involved? The geographic study area for my research is in New England. However, for similar environmental outcomes, research on nitrogen and other nonpoint source pollution would be applicable.

   Would studying the same problem in a new geographic region provide insight into the problem?

3. What focus group was applied?

   Would a different demographic group offer new information?

4. What data were used?

   Would insights emerge with a different dataset—collected differently or with different variables?

5. What are the theories involved? In my nitrogen example, one theory is that best management practices (BMP) reduce the total daily nitrogen load into the receiving waters. Another theory is that reducing the total daily maximum load (TDML) into the receiving waters improves water quality over time. Yet another theory is that the biogeochemical nutrient cycling is a watershed scale process.

Assessment

Review of your work remains a common theme. The research concept and ultimately the research proposal are not exceptions. Proposals have some standard review criteria that advisors, expert reviewers, and panels for funding agencies use to assess their merits. One part of this is whether the research should be conducted and whether it can be conducted in the manner stated. Your responsibility as an investigator is to write a document that addresses explicitly why the research needs to be conducted and how you will do it. That answer to the *why* question needs to be addressed here and now—before the specific research question even emerges. Writing the specifics on how you will conduct your work is saved for Chapter 11.

The research is assessed based on three primary criteria: novelty, relevance, and doability. Your goal is to come up with an idea that meets all three. Novelty of the work addresses whether the work is advancing science by answering a question with an answer yet unknown. One is to ask whether the work proposed is novel and advancing science. Novelty means it has not been done before. Some research is incremental, a small step away from what has been done before. Other research is more transformatitive by moving far past what is already known.

Inherently imbedded in novelty is whether it *matters* whether the question is even asked. Knowing for example whether there is a relationship between X and Y when that relationship is irrelevant is not a justifiable reason for the question. Relevance means it is meaningful in some way to society or science. To argue for funding that contributes both to society and science, Stokes (1997) categorized research into pure basic research, pure applied research, and use-inspired research. Pure basic research contributes to science, but the application for use in society is not yet apparent. Pure applied research contributes to society in a meaningful way but does not advance science, using the inventions by Thomas Edison as an example. Use-inspired research, in which Louis Pasteur is the exemplar, has a fundamental contribution to science but also has immediate application for society. Pasteur's research contributed to the science of chemistry and microbiology with immediate application to society with understanding diseases and pasteurized dairy products.

The third assessment is to ask whether the proposed activities are doable. Can the work be performed at all—and in the allotted time? Doability means the project you describe can be done with the resources and the time frame stated. This often results in what seems to be small, incremental steps. For example, a doable project is to discover the outcome of a model with a new dataset or in a new study area. This answers the question of how the same problem in a new geographic setting compares to what is known elsewhere. There is an assumption that there is something unique in the new setting such as environmental, political, demographic, or economic conditions. The knowledge gained from this project is new, incremental, and not particularly innovative. Harder research to conceptualize and implement is transformative research. This type of contribution transforms general thinking from how people operate now to something new. Most transformative research introduces new ways of conceptualizing a problem and is theoretically based. While featuring seemingly massive leaps, the researchers have taken the steps incrementally by using and applying ideas from other fields and adapting them or shifting them to the problem solved locally.

Transformative research advances theory. The theory influences the way we conceptualize or think about something. This goes back to the theoretical framework and the paradigm shifts discussed in Chapter 7 on the literature review. Some classic examples of transformative research are the following:

Relativity. Albert Einstein's theory—measurements are relative to the observer in both space and time.

Gravity. The force that one body acts upon the other is relative to the mass.

Plate tectonics. Describes the movement of the Earth's oceanic and continental crust.

Structure of DNA. The strand of molecules that forms genetic information is in the shape of a double helix.

The mission to produce transformative research explains the popularity in multidisciplinary or transdisciplinary research. Transdisciplinary research facilitates broad thinking and ideas generated from multiple disciplinary points of view. While transformative research is an aspirational goal for one's career, it is unusual for it to emerge from a PhD dissertation. In other words, no need to worry if your dissertation research is a small incremental step rather than massively transformative.

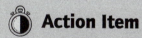

Action Item

Go to the website of a national funding agency, (e.g., National Science Foundation or National Institute of Health) and search the recently funded proposals. Examine how they have met the criteria for novelty, relevance, and doability.

Alternatively or additionally, look at the recently defended proposals by graduate students in your program. Assess these proposals for novelty, relevance, and doability.

In a sentence or two describe the motivation for your research. This addresses why your problem is important to solve.

Revise and Resubmit

The pathways to the research concept assume that both active reading and writing are part of the process. Here I describe the important activity of this chapter—revising and resubmitting the AOS. The AOS, which describes the boundaries of your research interests, needs to have more specificity. Since first writing this document, you have read and written about the literature much more extensively and have developed writing and revising skills that need to be practiced. Revisiting the AOS is also a tool to help you decide what research concept interests you.

The content from the AOS was knowledge you had about a small segment of the literature. It was material you either knew before you started (and what perhaps got you interested in graduate school to start) or what you read specifically to write the AOS. Since writing that document however you have read and written about a considerably larger body of literature. It is time to revisit the content of the AOS and incorporate new content into your AOS document.

From the writing guidelines in Chapter 6 and the experience writing the literature review, you have more skills for writing a more substantive (but not necessarily longer) AOS. One of the important ways to improve your writing is to write and rewrite. As a reminder, the tools for rewriting are the following:

Grammar: proper usage of the English language

Structure: the organization of the document, paragraph, and sentence

Content: the message of each sentence, paragraph, and the overall document

Format: consistency—paragraph tabulation, font, references

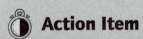 **Action Item**

Reread and critique your AOS. Using the tools in the writing toolbox, analyze the grammar, structure, content, and format of the document.

Rewrite the AOS into one that formulates a generalized research concept. The first paragraph should draw from your answers to the questions of what, how, and why.

Reminders

- Different pathways can lead to the research concept.
- Application, methods, theory.
- Research needs to be novel, relevant, and doable.
- Your research questions will become a particular instance of a general problem area you define.

References

Kamler, B., & Thomson, P. (2006). *Helping doctoral students write: Pedagogies for supervision.* New York: Routledge.

Stokes, D. E. (1997). *Pasteur's quadrant: Basic science and technological innovation.* Washington, DC: Brookings Institution Press.

10

Problem Statement

Introduction

The previous chapter developed a generalized research concept. The goal now is to write a specific instance of that generalized concept as a research objective or question. This specific instance becomes the basis for your research statement or problem statement. This chapter helps you generate a document that includes a research objective or question and the motivation for why the research needs to be conducted. The problem statement drills farther down the spiral from a research topic toward a solution you work toward in your dissertation (see Figure 10.1).

The terms *research statement* and *research problem* are used interchangeably in this chapter. Both terms refer to a specific instance of a generalized research goal within your area of specialization. The idea that you are solving a "problem" suggests the problem can be "solved." In many cases, research results do not necessarily solve the problem but rather contribute to understanding it better.

There are two distinguishable ways to describe the topic you are going to address: as an objective and as a question. A research objective describes a desired result or product. A research question seeks an answer through information or insight. Some argue that any research question can be phrased as a research objective and vice versa; others remain fixed that only certain types of research can fall into one or the other category. I separate the descriptions here and leave it to you (plus your advisor and committee) to decide which is more appropriate for your work.

The second feature of the research statement is an argument describing why your objective or question is important. You need to demonstrate that your problem has merit. Some argue that a good reason is simply because it is unknown. However, trivial questions lack merit. For example, the relationship between the number of people owning white cars and cancer incidents may be unknown. Unless there is merit, such as a reasonable hypothesis that owning a white car leads to cancer (or a cure), this relationship is trivial. So you do need to justify why the unknown subject is relevant and important.

Figure 10.1   Research spiral showing the research objective or question near the point of the spiral.

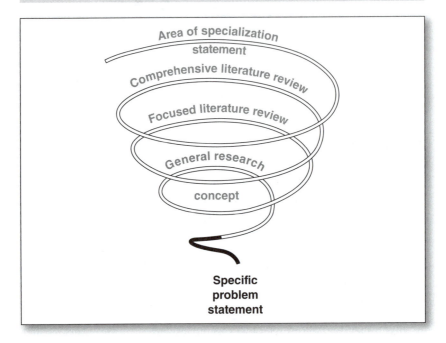

The third feature is to imagine the problem statement as a bridge that links the literature review (the unknown questions or emerging objectives) to the research methods (how the problem will be answered). There is an indication of both in your statement. As you think about the specifics of your research question(s) or objective(s) be sure to imagine this bridge (see Figure 10.2).

This chapter begins with a description of the two ways to express a problem statement: the research objective or the research question. These ideas are defined and reasons for picking one form over the other are stated. The next section addresses how to write and evaluate a research objective or question. Several activities, built mostly around the research question, allow students to practice evaluating research questions. Finally, the chapter ends with guidelines on how to write a problem statement that includes a specific research objective or question.

Ways to Describe the Research Problem

There are two ways to describe a research problem. One is through a research objective, which is a statement on what you plan to do. The second is through

Figure 10.2   The problem statement acts as a link, or bridge, between the literature review and methods.

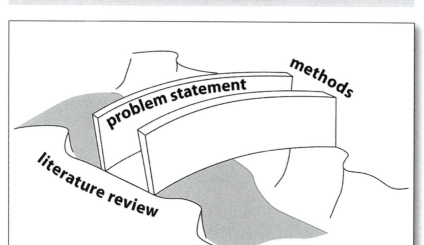

a research question. The form you select depends on the type of project you have in mind and the norms of your discipline, academic unit, and advisor. The last subsection addresses the role of hypothesis formation and testing relative to research questions.

RESEARCH OBJECTIVE

A research objective is a declarative statement describing an outcome-based goal investigating facts, theories, or methods. The outcome is a better understanding into a gap identified in the literature review.

Research objectives are more effectively used when the research topic involves developing a new method or describing a new theory or theoretical framework. For example, one of my colleagues develops new methods for locating alternative energy refueling stations (Kuby et al., 2009). His objective is to figure out the best places to put as few refueling stations as possible to serve as many customers as possible. Much of what he does is based on designing, developing, and testing new approaches to performing this task. While tasks such as this could be formulated into a question, it can be awkward when they turn into non–hypothesis generating questions. This is often true when the methods you expect to use are not directly statistical and based on hypothesis testing.

One challenge with writing a research objective is to clarify what component of it is *research* and not simply a task that does not advance knowledge or understanding. The research objective needs to solve a problem or gain new insight, not just perform a task. For example,

> The goal of my research is to design, create, and test a website for showing the locations of ATMs in Tempe, Arizona.

At the time this research objective was written, the idea of having ATM locations on a digital map was a new concept. No one (to our knowledge) had created such a website. Nevertheless, it did not advance scientific research because the methods (essentially, creating a digital map) were known. Instead, we revised the objective to read:

> The goal of my research is to design a framework for an interactive website that maps consumer services tested with an implementation on ATMs in Tempe, Arizona.

The difference between the two objectives is subtle, but the latter reflects a research need (a framework for interactive digital mapping) that can be created and evaluated with a case study (ATMs in Tempe, Arizona).

Evaluating a research objective or question involves the same steps. These steps involve critiquing the scientific merit of the objective and feasibility of the methods. The scientific merit is evaluated by determining whether there is a contribution to the literature. The feasibility is determined by examining the methods. The objective statement therefore needs to act as a bridge between the literature and methods.

RESEARCH QUESTION

The research question is an interrogative statement. Forming a research question is often identified as the initial step in the scientific method. The scientific method refers to a specific approach for investigating a problem or acquiring new knowledge.

The scientific method is expected to be objective, free from opinions, ideas, and biases of the human investigator. The scientific method is an approach for testing and modifying a research hypothesis through systematic data collection and experimental methods. The method is rooted in the formulation of a testable hypothesis derived from a research question.

A hypothesis describes a possible answer to the research question. To be a hypothesis in the scientific method framework, it must be testable through observation and experimental methods. Therefore the hypothesis comes prior to observation and experiment. The hypothesis is sometimes considered an educated guess and is derived from your experience with prior research, either your own or what you have read in the scientific literature.

The types of questions you pose can be descriptive, identify relationships, and suggest or prove causality. As questions move from description to causality, it implies more is known about the phenomenon as an interacting process. For example, early research on the urban heat island effect was descriptive. The research served to describe the presence of warmer nighttime temperatures in urban areas compared to outlying areas (Hucheon, Johnson, Lowry, Black, & Hadley, 1967). Later research focused on identifying the structural characteristics of the city that influence the urban heat island (Oke, 1981). Finally, nuances of the urban heat island effect, such as spatial patterns of land covers and the dynamics of energy fluxes, are now the focus of investigation (Masson, 2000).

Descriptive

When little is known about a subject, descriptive research questions provide initial insight into a particular phenomenon. Descriptive questions often begin with *what, who, where,* and *when*. They provide an answer with an account of a particular event, phenomenon, or person(s). The following are descriptive questions:

What was the impact of Hurricane Katrina on Mardi Gras attendance?

When did the floodwater recede from New Orleans?

Who in New Orleans was most and least affected by Hurricane Katrina?

Where did Hurricane Katrina evacuees go (and did they return)?

Most advisors will not be satisfied with a dissertation proposal that includes only a descriptive research question. Answering these questions does, however, provide a starting point for addressing why an issue is important, and potentially key relationships will emerge.

Relationship

Many relationship-based research questions are derived from descriptive questions and are motivated by aiming to understand the causes of the phenomenon being studied. The word *relationship* can even appear in the question:

What is the relationship between something and something else?

The word *relationship* here suggests a correlation between two variables (the *something* and the *something else*). A variable is a characteristic of a person, place, or thing. It takes on a nominal, ordinal, interval, or ratio value. One variable is what you want to study and the other influences it, ideally in some predicable way. Variables are examined further in Chapter 11 (Research Methods). Here's an example of a relationship question using variables:

> What is the relationship between urban surface temperatures and the spatial pattern of impervious surfaces?

This type of question does not suggest causation. That is saved for causal research questions discussed next. Think correlation not causation when forming (or answering) relationship-related research questions.

An interesting sidebar here relates to exploratory data analysis and data mining, analytical techniques assuming no a priori knowledge. Relationship research questions assume you have a priori knowledge about the two variables. You are testing a hypothesis that this relationship does or does not exist. More details on exploratory data analysis, data mining, and hypothesis testing are provided in Chapter 11.

Causal

The goal of a causal research question is to test a hypothesis based on a cause-then-effect outcome. The objective is to move beyond a simple relationship between two variables toward a relationship based on one affecting the other positively or negatively. Unfortunately, because of complexity in the world, the direct cause and effect may not be confirmed. Nonetheless, because researchers aim to solve a problem or predict an outcome (not just understand it), they strive to understand causality.

This type of question is similar to those that describe relationships but often has a stronger implication of which variable is the driver. For example, compare these two questions:

> What is the relationship between urban surface temperatures and the spatial pattern of impervious surfaces?
>
> How has the increase of impervious surfaces from 1970 to 2000 affected urban surface temperature?

The first one aims to determine if there is a relationship between the two variables (urban surface temperature and impervious surfaces); the second question implies the relationship exists and aims to determine the strength and pattern of the relationship. In this example, it is fairly easy to determine causality because warming urban temperatures do not generate impervious surfaces. Another process (human based) drives the development of impervious surfaces. Furthermore, other urban surfaces (e.g., buildings, grass, water) also affect surface temperature, and the complexity of these variables needs to be considered in the analysis. These are discussed further in Chapter 11.

HYPOTHESES

Testable hypotheses are the engine of the scientific research method. If you are using statistical methods, you rely on the creation of a hypothesis and an alternative hypothesis and then use specific methods to test them. You typically develop these hypotheses when you create your research questions. The hypotheses provide yet another strong link (part of the bridge) to the research methods.

A hypothesis, which is sometimes called the alternative hypothesis, is a statement that can be verified (true or not true) reflecting an answer to your research question. You first create a null hypothesis, which is not proven itself but leaves you to select the alternative hypothesis. The alternative hypothesis is the relationship you want to prove.

A null hypothesis, sometimes referred to as H_O, is the default hypothesis. More simply put, the null hypothesis is typically formed by embedding the word *not* into the alternative hypothesis. As a scientist, your role is to reject or fail to reject the null hypothesis. If the null hypothesis is rejected, then the alternative hypothesis is true. When you fail to reject the null hypothesis, the alternative hypothesis fails. The null hypothesis can never be tested or proven to be true; it merely indicates a different hypothesis (whether it is your alterative hypothesis or not) is needed to explain the phenomenon.

When statistical methods are part of your analysis, hypothesis statements should be included with your research question. Typically, the null hypothesis (H_0) is not needed. For example, from an earlier question,

What is the relationship between urban surface temperatures and the spatial pattern of impervious surfaces?

H_1: Clusters of impervious surfaces lead to higher urban surface temperatures.

This statement can be tested against a null hypothesis, which is then rejected or not rejected.

Two other terms worth mentioning here are Type I and Type II errors. A Type I error is a false positive in your result. In other words, you reject the null hypothesis based on your statistical test, suggesting that the alternative hypothesis is true. But since the statistical test is in error, the alterative hypothesis is not true. For example, you take a pregnancy test and the test says "pregnant" when you are in fact not pregnant.

A Type II error is a false negative. In statistical terms, you have failed to reject the null hypothesis and therefore cannot accept the alterative hypothesis. In this case, however, the alterative hypothesis is true. Returning to the previous example, the pregnancy test says "not pregnant," but you are in fact pregnant.

Both Type I and Type II errors depend on the formulation of null hypotheses. The relationship between the hypotheses and outcomes is easily visualized in Table 10.1. The causes and consequences of Type I and Type II errors are discussed in Chapter 11 on methods.

The following series of tasks will help you write and evaluate effective research questions. Even if you envision your work as objective, these exercises build skills for effective evaluation of narrow, doable, and nontrivial research questions.

Table 10.1   Relationship between Type I and Type II errors and hypothesis statements.

	Null Is True	**Null Is False**
Reject null hypothesis	Type I error (false positive)	Outcome correct (true positive)
Fail to reject null hypothesis	Outcome correct (true negative)	Type II error (false negative)

Evaluating Research Objectives and Questions

Forming a statement or question is relatively easy. However, determining whether it is specific enough and has merit is more difficult. This section gives you tools to write and evaluate research questions. The focus is directed specifically at research questions (and not the objective), but the ideas are easily extended to research objectives.

The following exercises are designed to help you formulate and evaluate a specific instance of your research concept. Some of them (such as Roll-a-Research) are fun to do with a group, like your dissertation support group.

ROLL-A-RESEARCH[1]

While the research questions or objectives alone are just a few lines of text, they are often written and rewritten multiple times. To understand why, you need skills to evaluate the merit of written questions (objectives). This activity asks you to write many hypothetical research questions (not objectives) and evaluate them in terms of importance, knowledge in the literature, and feasibility. If your subject area warrants a research objective instead of a question, you should evaluate the merit of the objective in the same manner these questions are evaluated. This exercise moves you outside your area of

---

[1]This in-class activity was designed by Randall Cerveny.

specialization and therefore outside your known literature. It is fine to speculate on these topics—just do your best.

1. Obtain a pair of dice or use an online dice-rolling program.

Using the table as a guide, generate the parameters of your research question by rolling your dice five times. This will generate a sequence of numbers and correspond to the Place, Geographic Scale, Temporal Scale, Topic, and Containing Word or Phrase categories.

Table 10.2 Roll-a-Research framework.

Roll Number	Place	Geographic Scale	Temporal Scale	Topic	Containing Word or Phrase
2	Asia	10 m–100 m (~10 yds.–100 yds.) [local]	Last hundred years	Hurricanes	"Compare(d) to"
3	Africa	1 km–100 km (~1/2 mi.–60 mi.) [city]	Seasonal	Urban city development	"What if"
4	Europe	100 km–1,000 km (60 mi.–600 mi.) [regional]	Weekday vs. weekend	Education	"What would happen"
5	Global	Continental	Last 5 years	Changing economies (e.g., rust belt cities)	"How has"
6	South America	Global	Monthly	Transportation/subways	"Contrast"
7	North America	**Choice**	**Choice**	**Choice**	**Choice**

(Continued)

Table 10.2   (Continued)

Roll Number	Place	Geographic Scale	Temporal Scale	Topic	Containing Word or Phrase
8	Australia	10 m–100 m (~10 yds.–100 yds.) [local]	Next year	Migration (people or animals)	"Is" (starting word)
9	Asia	1 km–100 km (~1/2 mi.–60 mi.) [city]	Daily / diurnal	Media/ communications	"Change"
10	North America	100 km–1,000 km (60 mi.–600 mi.) [regional]	Last 50 years	Invasive plants/ animals/ Species (e.g., tamarisk)	"Has" (starting word)
11	Pacific Islands	Continental	Holiday vs. "normal" day	Recreation (rafting)	"Compare(d) to"
12	Antarctica	Global	Next 5 years	Environmental impact	"Why"

For the first roll, write down the place for your research (Column 2). The second roll determines the geographic scale (Column 3); third roll the temporal scale (Column 4); fourth roll the topic (Column 5); and the fifth roll the containing word or phrase (Column 6).

If in five rolls you produce a sequence such as 5, 11, 5, 9, and 2, your resulting parameters are the following:

5	11	5	9	2
Global →	Continental →	Last 5 years →	Media/ communications →	"Compare(d) to"

These parameters form the basis or framework for your research question. With this information, write six research questions, such as these two:

Compared to the years 2001–2005, how has Facebook communication changed the way people living on different continents share political information in the last five years (2008–2012)?

Compared to e-mail exchange, what has been the trend in cross-continental exchange of standard mail in the last 5 years?

Note that for any given sequence of numbers generated from five rolls, there are many possible research questions. Note too that there are millions of combinations of rolls possible, giving you endless possibilities for generating research questions. However, some roll sequences generate parameters that do not provide you a framework for a plausible research question. For example, consider this, 12, 8, 11, 2, 5, which produces this:

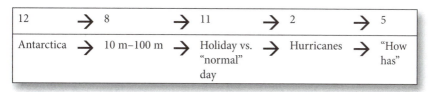

You can create a question from this type of series:

How have hurricanes that have fallen on holidays affected snowfall in Antarctica in small-area (10 m) distributions versus those that have fallen on "normal" days?

But even without being an Antarctica or hurricane expert, you know the theory in the literature does not support this question. Throw out this sequence and roll again.

For the next exercise, write down at least six questions per sequence. Generate at least six sequences so that you write 36 research questions. Compare them and select the one you think is best based on the following evaluation criteria:

- Can the bridge between the literature review and the methods be envisioned?
- Scope. Is the problem sufficiently specific?
- Testability. Is there a working hypothesis that can be tested?
- Doability. Can the necessary data be collected?
- Explainability. Does the question provide insight into a phenomenon?

A matrix such as that in Table 10.3 helps systematically compare the questions. Consider this example:

Sequence: South America (6), City (3), Holiday vs. "normal" day (11), environmental impact (12), "Is" (8)

Now rank each column from 1 to 3, where 0 = unacceptable, 1 = poor, 2 = okay, and 3 = good. Include comments when necessary. The sum of the column rows is reflected in the Evaluation column, enabling you to objectively rank the questions.

Table 10.3 Sample matrix for evaluating research questions.

Question	Bridge	Scope	Testability	Doability	Explainability	Evaluation
Is there an environmental impact on cities in South America during holidays?	1 Could provide insight on environmental impact of holidays but too broad to know the methods	0 Lacks specificity in definition: environmental impact, which cities, and which holidays	1 A hypothesis could be generated, but it would not be testable.	0 No specifics on methods	1 Maybe, but too hard to evaluate	3 Okay
Is the air quality in South American cities better on holiday or "normal" weekends?	2 It implies that air quality is related to holidays, presumably due to travel.	1 No specificity on which cities should be considered or what is considered a holiday weekend	1 Given the tie to the literature on travel during holiday weekends, there could be a hypothesis that holiday weekends have better air quality because people aren't doing errands.	1 The researcher would need to guess which cities and which holiday weekends should be considered.	3 Good	8 An improvement over the previous question but still lacks sufficient detail

Question	Bridge	Scope	Testability	Doability	Explainability	Evaluation
	2	3	3	3	2	13
Is the relative volume of rubbish produced during Carnival in Buenos Aires related to the economic revenue generated compared to "normal" weekends?	Relationship between rubbish and economy not clear Need to quantify both economic revenue and trash volume	Good specifics	Testable hypothesis can be created	Providing data are available on the weekend basis	Insight on trash and economy is unclear	Good because of the specifics provided
	1	1	2	0	2	6
Is a smaller city in Brazil relatively more vulnerable to environmental diseases compared to larger cities?	Since the question lacks a temporal scope, the tie to the literature is unclear.	Lacks temporal scope. When is the study being considered? Lacks the specific cities to be investigated; which environmental diseases	A hypothesis could be tested, but it would be based on an incomplete research question.	Not enough detail provided	Insight could be generated	With just a few more details this could be a good question, but it is harder to see how holidays would factor in.

(Continued)

141

Table 10.3 (Continued)

Question	Bridge	Scope	Testability	Doability	Explainability	Evaluation
Is the water quality of South American cities with a population >300,000 worse on Christmas Day compared to "normal" days?	1 What? Why Christmas and water quality? Maybe there is more swimming. Test would be better a day or so after a holiday instead of that day.	3 Specifics are provided.	1 A testable hypothesis can be formulated.	0 Not possible to acquire the necessary data; too many cities.	1 Unclear link between the specific holiday and the phenomenon being studied.	6 While the specifics are provided, it does not necessarily result in a strong research question.
Is there an increase in waterborne diseases in the 3 days following summer holidays compared to the three days following "normal" days in Caracas?	3 Plausible link between swimming on holidays and when diseases appear	3 Scope sufficiently described	3 A clear testable hypothesis can be formed.	3 Data can be collected and analyzed.	3 Insight into when waterborne diseases may be spread	15 Best of the best (but you might come up with something better still).

From each sequence (six total) use the Evaluation column (sum of columns 2–5) in Table 10.3 to help select the best question. Keep this best-of-the-best question on hand for future activities.

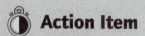

Action Item

Practice identifying research questions and the linkages between them and the literature and methods.

1. What is the name of your discipline's flagship journal?
2. From one issue, select two articles not in your primary subject area.
3. Identify the research question the articles either state directly (some articles do) or that you infer based on the article.
4. What literature do the articles support in their question?
5. What approach do the articles take to solving the problem?
6. Evaluate these questions based on the matrix in Table 10.3. Can you improve their question?

A Specific Research Topic

The last section of this chapter contains two Action Items designed to help you create your research question. Using the gaps in knowledge from the literature review you wrote and the evaluation tools described earlier, write your own research objective or question.

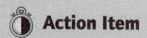

Action Item

Create your own research question or objective. The columns in Table 10.3 help specify and frame your research question from the general to the specific. Using your research concept as a guide, answer the following questions about your research topic:

What is the geographic location (e.g., place) associated with your research?

What is the target group?

(Continued)

(Continued)

What is the geographic scale?

What is the temporal scale?

What is the topic?

Using the phrases in the Containing Word or Phrase column, write as many possible research questions on your topic as possible and evaluate each of them on scientific merit and feasibility. If necessary, change the other parameters (e.g., temporal scale) and assess how that affects your questions.

The problem statement is more than just a research question or objective. It is a short document ranging from 500 to 1,500 words. When embedded in your proposal, it should be situated between the end of the literature review and the beginning of your methods (and probably edited to closer to 500 words). Remember that it is the bridge between two important pieces: the literature review and the methods. There will be elements to your problem statement that tie to the literature. There will also be hints on what kinds of methods you will use. Neither is described in detail in the document you write, but both are suggested. The document you write here instead needs to identify which pieces of the literature are important and provide an approach on how you will solve the problem.

⏱ To Do List

Research topic → General research topic or question → Specific research question

1. Return to one of your best research questions from Roll-a-Research. Even without knowing the literature or the methods typically used in this area, look at the question and consider what they may be. Envision how this is a bridge.

2. Write down your own topic, probably from your AOS or literature review.

3. Write down several general research areas that emerged from your literature review.

4. Use Roll-a-Research to formulate 10 questions in your topic area.

5. Evaluate each based on the matrix in Table 10.3.

6. Select the best of the best and determine if it is a realistic research question you can use in your proposal.

Consider your best question in terms of the following:

1. Can you see the bridge in the question between the literature and methods?

2. Are the prospective methods doable?

3. Do you have the skills to do it?

4. Do you have the data or the ability to collect the data (pilot studies can help here)?

5. If you explained your question to your mother, would she understand it?

6. Will you know when the research is complete?

7. How does it deal with theory, method, and domain/application?

8. Does it cover the problem you want to solve?

Here are some concerns with problem statements:

1. They are too small and too trivial.

   How many cars does the Desert Vista Mall have visiting it?

   You know how to answer this question. You know which mall to visit and what to do. The problem with this question is that it does not address what is important in the literature. This question could be important for the transportation planning literature however and could be rephrased to reflect that. The question is improved by relating it to weekend or weekday traffic or which mall entrance has more or less traffic.

2. They are too large and not doable.

   How do we improve reading in elementary schools?

   This question ties clearly into the research area of elementary school success by researching reading in general, but it lacks any link to the research methods. The question could be improved by asking how different intervention programs help struggling students or how curricula at charter schools differ from public schools.

3. They can be answered yes or no (while some yes-or-no questions are actually okay, they need to be testing something specific).

Can remote sensing be used to detect impervious surfaces?

This is a weak yes-or-no question. There is a link to both the literature review (the need to detect impervious surfaces) and the approach (remote sensing), but both pieces lack specificity. You can improve the question by adding details to both:

Can Markov random fields improve classification of impervious surfaces in Quickbird imagery compared to maximum likelihood classifiers in desert cities?

This is an example of a strong yes-or-no question. On the literature side it suggests a history of detecting impervious surfaces with maximum-likelihood classification approaches. On the methods side, it suggests the approach will use Markov random fields methods in an unspecified desert city.

The problem statement will eventually be embedded in your proposal, ideally after the literature review. At this stage, however, you should write a short freestanding document describing your research goals to share with your committee. Since it is a freestanding document, you need to include a small statement describing your topic and why it is important. This is an opportunity to write your topic and the existing literature into a concise but specific statement.

🕐 To Do List

The problem statement (this activity) expands on your research question(s) by answering the following questions:

What are you studying (the topic)?

Why is it important to solve? (Who cares about this?)

How have others tried to understand your topic (indication of past methods)?

How do you envision addressing it differently (nonspecific hint on your methods)?

Remember that the problem statement is a bridge between the literature review and methods and should have hints and insights into both. Be sure to refer back to gaps in the literature and questions that remain or emerge because of the literature. Likewise, identify the approach you will take to solving the problem differently.

Obtain feedback. Share your ideas first with your dissertation support group and advisor. Also extend your ideas to your committee (use your whole village). Perhaps prepare a 5-minute or longer oral presentation describing your ideas. (See Chapter 13 for ideas on oral presentations.) In your presentation, remember that the problem statement should have sufficient information about both the literature you draw from and the methods you expect to use in order to be a stand-alone document your committee members can evaluate (the bridge). This might even be an effective time to have a preproposal meeting with your entire committee.

Reminders

- Consider research questions and research objectives.
- Evaluate each prospective question or objective based on novelty and feasibility.
- Explain why your question or objective is an important problem to solve.
- Speak with advisors and peers for feedback.

References

Hucheon, R. J., Johnson, R. H., Lowry, W. P., Black, C. H., & Hadley, D. (1967). Observations of urban heat island in a small city. *Bulletin of the American Meteorological Society, 48*(1), 7–8.

Kuby, M., Lines, L., Schultz, R., Xie, Z., Kim, J.-G., & Lim, S. (2009). Optimization of hydrogen stations in Florida using the flow-refueling location model. *International Journal of Hydrogen Energy, 34*(15), 6045–6064. doi:10.1016/j.ijhydene.2009.05.050

Masson, V. (2000). A physically-based scheme for the urban energy budget in atmospheric models. *Boundary-Layer Meteorology, 94*(3), 357–397. doi:10.1023/A:1002463829265

Oke, T. R. (1981). Canyon geometry and the nocturnal urban heat-island—Comparison of scale model and field observations. *Journal of Climatology, 1*(3), 237–254.

11

Research Methods

Introduction

The problem statement as described in the previous chapter provides a view into the research methods. That is, it suggests what activities the investigator plans to undertake to complete a research objective or answer a research question. The research methods section of a proposal moves from those hints to describe the approach with specificity, enabling the reader to know exactly where and how the problem will be addressed. The methods part of the proposal is extremely important and, oddly enough, often not put together well. Too many people think, "I'll just figure it out as I go along." That will not be sufficient with an advisor, at a dissertation proposal defense, or for external funding. So your best bet is to learn how to do it now.

Research methods (typically those involving a research question) typically have three main sections: a description of the study area or scope, the data needed and how those data will be acquired, and the approach to analyze the data. This organization tends to differ for a research project that develops and tests new theories or methods (often associated with a research objective). These feature two main sections, a detailed description of the new approach (theory, method, technique, model) and how the effectiveness of the new approach will be evaluated.

This chapter first describes the content of the five sections just mentioned. Following that are a few activities to help identify different methods and evaluate their effectiveness with research questions. The chapter concludes with several key points in preparing your own methods statement.

Methods to Answer a Research Question

Most proposals with a research question have three main sections to the methods: study area or scope, data acquisition, and procedures. The first describes how your research is bounded, either geographically or conceptually. The second describes how the data will be acquired. The last section describes how you will use those data to answer your research question. Here each section and the rationale for why they are needed are described.

STUDY AREA OR SCOPE

Will your study take place in Argentina or Brazil? Will you interview planners or councilmembers? Answering these questions defines either the study area (where) or your scope (who). In some cases both need to be answered, such as for planners and councilmembers in 14 towns in Connecticut. In addition, readers expect a rationale for why the study area or scope identified is reasonable for the research. In statistical terms, the rationale describes why the sample identified is representative of the total population.

The study area statement begins with a very specific definition of the bounding region of your study. This could be municipal boundaries, watershed boundaries, specific coordinates (e.g., longitude and latitude), or any other description that outlines the extent of your study. Conventionally, investigators include a map outlining the study area (see Figure 11.1). Subsequent statements describe the physical or social characteristics of the region.

Subsequent statements support why the study area you selected makes sense relative to your research question. Research questions on the causes and consequences of dust storms need to be studied in a geographic region where frequent dust storms occur (to find the causes) and where the consequences matter (e.g., near cities). In this example, the investigator would describe the physical conditions of the area that make dust storms possible and how dust storms impact human populations (e.g., safety issues due to reduced visibility, health problems).

In many social science research projects, the scope of the research is more critical than the geographic region. For example, research may involve acquiring data from a social networking website such as Facebook or Twitter to study the connectedness of a certain music style. In this example, stating that the study area is the whole globe is less relevant than describing why the social networking website selected appropriately represents the population of social networkers. This would require some explanation that people who listen to a specific genre of music also participate enough in the social networking site selected.

The worst reason you can use to describe why a certain study area or scope was selected is "because I had access to the data." This may be how you stumbled into the project, but it does not justify why it is a good area for your investigation. Like the earlier example from Phoenix, Arizona, would also be a good study site for dust storm research because of the physical conditions (dry and strong winds) and the historical problem of air quality in the area. The reason for selecting Phoenix would not be "because I live there."

Figure 11.1   An example of the study area for a research project. The figure shows both the general research location (City of Tempe within Arizona) and the specific locations where data were collected (point locations of apartment complexes). Image taken from Wentz et al. (in press).

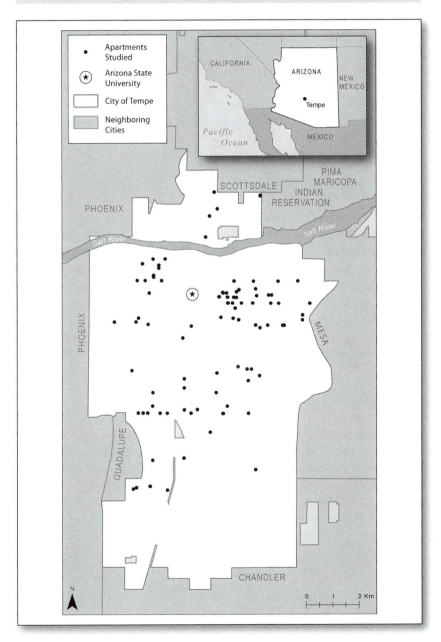

Remember, when describing the study or scope of your research, you are answering two basic questions:

1. What is the specific extent or scope of your study?

2. What makes this area or scope appropriate for the research question?

The section itself does not need to be long. In research proposals and the related referred journal articles, it is typically a few paragraphs at most.

In evaluating your study area or scope, you should consider how it might lead to either Type I or Type II errors. Recall that a Type I error is when your results reject the null hypothesis when it is actually true; a Type II error is when your results do not reject the null hypothesis when they should. For example, whether I select a subset of Phoenix without residential pools or with numerous community pools, my results would not show the effect of pools on residential water consumption.

DATA

In the study area or scope section, you described the boundaries of the study. The data section of the proposal states exactly what data contained within this boundary will be used for the study. The data section also describes the plan for how these data will be acquired. Generally speaking, the first paragraph of the data section names each variable in your study. Subsequent paragraphs describe the specifics of each variable, including the measurement level, the number of observations, and how they will be acquired.

A variable represents an attribute or characteristic of the phenomenon studied, identified as either dependent or independent. The dependent variable represents the phenomenon you are studying, the variable you are observing. The independent variable is that which you hypothesize controls the changes and differences observed in the dependent variable. For example, a change in the number (or size) of pools (independent variable) is hypothesized to change the amount of water consumed (dependent variable). While the terms *dependent variable* and *independent variable* are strongly associated with statistical methods, they are equally applicable to nonstatistical methods too.

The measurement level states what will be measured or observed for each observation you acquire. In the water consumption example, the research question may state a plan to analyze 2010 residential water consumption in the City of Phoenix. You make think it obvious what data are to be collected (obviously, residential water consumption in Phoenix for 2010), but at the top of the next page compare the two descriptions of the measurement level for these data.

For my study, I will obtain hourly household water consumption for the month of July 2010 from 300 randomly determined homes in Phoenix.

For my study, I will obtain total monthly water consumption for each U.S. census tract in the city of Phoenix for 2010.

Note the difference in these two measurement levels. The first will show hourly variation in water use; the second will show seasonal variation. Due to your research question (where the time span should be specified), the broad time span should be stated, but the more detailed (monthly or hourly and the specifics of July) time span needs to be stated too. The measurement level statement intuitively provides the number of observations, but you should state it explicitly to be sure. In the first example, it is stated (300 homes). In the second, it is implied (the total number of census tracts).

Research plans need to state how many observations will be acquired and subsequently analyzed. Proposal reviewers depend on this information to assess how well your sample is representative of your population as well as how reasonable it is to acquire the needed data. For example, primary interview data can be time-consuming to acquire—up to 3 hours or so per observation. Needed is a balance between an acceptable number of interviews for the research and the time needed to obtain them. If your proposal states you will have 200 interviews in hand, this will be viewed with a raised eyebrow or two. Conversely, two or three interviews will be equally suspect. If you are knowledgeable about your study area or scope, you can make a reasonable statement on how many observations you can expect to obtain.

Data are acquired through primary, secondary, or tertiary means. Primary data collection refers to data you collect yourself with known methods. Both secondary and tertiary data collection refer to data collected by someone else— the difference is whether the collection methods are known (secondary) or not known (tertiary).

Studies that acquire data through primary means need a description on how the data will be obtained. Some primary data collection methods are the following:

Instruments such as GPS, cameras, digital recorders

Collecting samples of soils, rocks, plants

Observations in shopping centers, city council meetings, parks

Interviews with people riding buses, in public buildings

Review of documents in public offices, historical archives

Surveys conducted online or in selected focus groups

Further description on data acquisition includes a discussion of the sampling strategies. How is the target observation identified? Is the sample random? What makes the data collected sufficient for answering your research questions?

When the data used are secondary or tertiary, the proposal needs to state the source of the data. This could be a reference to a government agency (e.g., city or county government), a private organization (e.g., the company Digital Globe distributes high-resolution satellite imagery), or a research group at a university. Secondary or tertiary data may be simple or challenging to acquire. Some data are easily downloaded from the Internet while others require permission from an agency or the individuals who collected the data.

In all cases where human subjects are part of the observation, researchers are required to submit data collection methods for review to avoid violating the rights and welfare of the research subjects. In the United States, universities (and other agencies where research is conducted) are mandated to have an Institutional Review Board (IRB) approve prior to data collection planned research that involves human subjects. Much of this involves making sure the participants are informed, their identities are protected, and they understand what they gain from participating. More details on the IRB and how to obtain its approval are presented in Chapter 2 (Ethics).

Evaluating your data definition and collection strategy requires a critical consideration of Type I and Type II errors, perhaps more so than when the study area was evaluated. These errors can occur because of the variables selected, the measurement level, and how they were acquired (e.g., sampling strategy or source). More evaluation strategies are listed shortly.

PROCEDURES

The last part of the methods section is a discussion of the procedures applied to the data collected. By this point, the reader will likely know if the work is qualitative, quantitative, or a mixed-method approach, but exactly which needs to be stated. Typically, research proposals engage in a combination of procedures, and each needs to be stated.

For quantitative approaches, begin by stating the technique and how each of the variables will be included. In such cases (unless space is severely limited), including the mathematical equations enhances the credibility of the proposal, even when the technique is well known, such as an ordinary least-squares regression model. For example, say you are analyzing the impact of a housing policy on poverty over time. This requires some measure of "poverty," which could be an index derived from a combination of variables such as literacy, access to health care, employment rate, and available transportation. The second part requires a description on how the index is analyzed over time. There are numerous time series analysis techniques. Some analyze seasonality (which doesn't make sense in this case), and others quantify long-term trends and temporal autocorrelation (which may apply). While other techniques may emerge as the data are analyzed, the plan needs to be described.

Research involving qualitative methods requires a similarly rigorous description of approach. You need to provide a statement on what method you will use. Regardless of which method you select, you need to describe how the method will be implemented with your problem context. If you have conducted interviews, how will you interpret them? For example, if you are using content analysis, what are the initial codes you will employ? What approach will you take to validate your coding?

More often than not, proposal reviews are returned with a comment that reads, "Not enough detail in the methods." Typically, this means there is not enough detail in the procedures. This is true with PhD proposal reviews as well as those for research funding. Part of the reason this happens so often is because writing about something you haven't yet done is hard. We want to figure out our methods as we go along, adapting as the problems and solutions emerge. However, obtaining permission from your advisor (or funding from the NSF) requires you to have a plan. It seems you need to have completed (or nearly) the research in order to write a detailed description of the methods.

The other type of pitfall to avoid in proposal writing is too much detail in the methods or, really, the wrong type of detail. While this problem is more prevalent in theses and dissertations, it happens in proposal writing as well. Typically, the problem isn't too much detail; instead, it is the type of detail provided. The wrong kind of detail describes the mechanics of doing the research and neglects to describe the specific approach. Think of the difference between the mechanics of the analysis and the approach as the difference between specific software steps and how those steps combine to form a whole conceptual step.

Return again to the issue of Type I and Type II errors. The wrong method, just like a poorly defined study area or inappropriately defined data, could lead to the wrong conclusion about your study. Consider here how alternative analytical procedures could impact your study.

Research Objective

The previous section described what to include for a research question. This section focuses on the other type of research: a research objective. A research project that involves designing, developing, and testing a theoretical framework or new method will not fit into the template for a research question. It can be forced into that template, but it does not work well because there are missing pieces. An alternative template, which does work, involves describing the new approach, how to develop it, and then how to evaluate it. The evaluation (particularly for new methods) defines the proposal as research. The reason the research question template partially works is because evaluating a new theory or method often involves a case study, which is tested much like a research question.

NEW APPROACH

The first step involves describing generically your approach. What I mean by *generically* here is a description independent of any specific case study or data you may use later to demonstrate or evaluate your approach. The reason for making the theory or method generic is because the ultimate goal is enabling the approach to be used in many case studies, independent from your specific case study. Your case study is part of your evaluation of the method or theory (the second step described here), not the description of the method or theory.

To create a generic description of a theoretical framework or new concept, you will likely need to define new terms or constructs included in your theory. A construct is an idealized entity or object that is part of your theory. The relationship between the constructs is then described by specific rules you define. These rules identify the ways one construct is linked or bounded to another. They can suggest influence or causality, which can then be demonstrated through a case study.

There may be a need to describe any possible outcomes associated with the theory. In many cases, a figure or graphic helps to visualize the relationships (see Figure 11.2). Since I tend to think and work quantitatively, this example reflects a flowchart-like appearance, but that is not always the case. Other formats are Venn diagrams, bubble charts, and other graphical ways to demonstrate constructs, linkages, and possibly flows.

Instead of a new theory or conceptual framework, your research may involve the design and testing of a new method. In the case of quantitative methods, the explanation of the approach may be as simple as providing an equation or two, with each of the variables explicitly defined. This includes the variables and the outcome. In the case of qualitative methods, the generic description requires the data or materials needed and what will be done with them. In both quantitative and qualitative cases, it is the proposal writer's responsibility to define the inputs (what anyone using your approach

Figure 11.2 Example of a generic theoretical relationship between constructs.

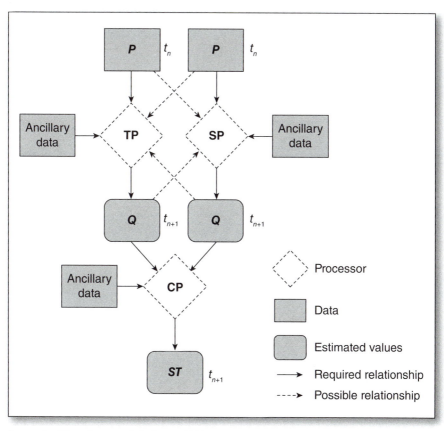

Source: See Wentz, Peuquet, & Anderson, 2010.

will need), what is done with the inputs (mathematical equations), and the results (the output).

IMPLEMENTATION AND EVALUATION

Demonstrating a new theory or implementing a new approach requires you to illustrate that it works or improves understanding compared to prior approaches. Implementing the new approach may involve creating a graphic to show the relationship between abstract ideas, writing a computer program, or building a mathematical or statistical model. In your proposal, state your plan on how it is to be implemented. For abstract models, you may need to have a draft already in place. For computer programs, mathematical models, and statistical models, you will need to provide the implementation environment (e.g., the software system) and know the primary variables and their relationships.

While your goal may be to develop and test a new theory or method, it is insufficient in most cases to apply it to a single study and declare that it works. Instead, your objective is to demonstrate not only that it works but also that it works better than any other method that aims to do the same thing. Part of your activity therefore involves defining what is meant by *better* and establishing a method for comparing your method based on those criteria.

Some of the ways to show a new approach is better are a case study, a series of examples, a comparative analysis, or a survey. A case study illustrates how the theory or method will produce anticipated relationships or results. A series of examples describes how the theory or approach would influence or act in a range of scenarios. A comparative study implements complementary approaches (e.g., other methods that aim to analyze data in a similar way) and compares the results of the different studies against a list of qualitative and quantitative criteria. A survey invites prospective users to interact with the theory or method and encourages feedback as to its effectiveness.

The methods part of your proposal needs to include specifics on the evaluation task. These research methods design elements are not determined "as you go along." For example, including a case study in your methods section requires you to describe why the case study is a good representation of your problem, what variables will be used, and how they will be analyzed. A comparative analysis requires you to have written a comparative table (see Table 11.1). A series of examples needs to identify the cross-section and topics of your examples. You also need to write your survey instrument, which includes your target sample, how you will recruit participants, and the questions you will ask in cases of a user assessment.

Developing these methods to decide what you mean by *better* involves returning to the literature to design your case study or write your survey. Consider what placed you along this path to finding a new approach. Was it that other methods used too many data sources? Was it that the theory did not explain certain observations? The idea of *better* may result in criteria that can be objectively or subjectively compared. In the proposal, all the comparison criteria need to be listed. The method for evaluating each also needs to be described. What is the new approach better than? Tables such as the following can be used to outline comparison criteria.

Your objective is inferential; that is, you want to be able to claim that your sample (e.g., your case study, examples) says something about the population

Table 11.1   Example of comparison criteria for a new method.

Objective	
Criteria	**Method for Comparison**
Runs faster	Compare the runtimes
Produces more accurate results	Compare model output to observations
Requires less data input	Count the number of data inputs
Subjective	
Liked better by users	User survey
Understood better by users	User survey
Is more intuitive to users	User survey

as a whole (that the method or theory can be generally applied). In Table 11.1, the new approach is clearly compared to one or more other methods, presumably existing and perhaps even widely used. Metrics may also simply evaluate the theory or method independently. Also note that criteria are separated by objective and subjective evaluation. In both objective and subjective cases the analytical methods (quantitative or qualitative) need to be described. Here, using the template from the Procedures section gives guidance on how to write this section. The key is to include specificity in your description; state details such as analysis of variance. Include the tools (both descriptive and inferential) used to evaluate your survey results.

While Type I and Type II errors do not directly apply since you are not using hypothesis testing in the same way you might be using statistical methods, it is still worth thinking through the outcomes of such errors. Consider here how the topic, study area, and data of your case study; the range of your examples; or the survey instrument might lead you to the wrong conclusion about your new theory or method.

Proposal Evaluation—Validity and Reliability

While the approaches mentioned describe how to evaluate a new theory or method, you also need to consider how to evaluate your methods as a whole. Some standard questions need to be answered to evaluate a research proposal. In particular, consider whether the project can be completed and whether the methods described will likely answer the research question posed. More systematically, however, validity and reliability are considered. Validity is an indication that the research methods are testing what is intended. Reliability considers the repeatability of the experiment.

The relationship between how and why something came to be and how it may change in the future, however, is tenuous, and the validity of the conclusions is brought into question. Trochim (2006) effectively explains this through external validity, construct validity, internal validity, and conclusion validity. My explanations here are drawn from ideas he presents. External validity relates to how data were sampled. Making statements from a study to a general population assumes the general population will respond the same way the study group does. The problem however is that the sample is never perfectly representative of the population—different times, places, cultures, and settings all factor in and make subtle changes. Construct validity is whether what you measured actually represents what you intend to study—and how effectively (reliability). This is problematic in cases of unknown interactions between variables that go unmeasured or are more socially based, such as when people are nervous about being interviewed. Internal validity refers to the design of the study. A single study may show the cause and effect between two or more variables, but other causes may provide alternative explanations not included in the study design. Finally, conclusion validity pertains to how conclusions were drawn because of the way they were analyzed. Two problems are when you determine a relationship exists when none does or when you determine a relationship does not exist when one actually does. These often relate to the statistical analysis performed. While I briefly summarized Trochim's explanations here, reading his book or visiting his website provides a much more extensive and informative discussion.

The second category for proposal evaluation is reliability. Reliability means that your study can be repeated and the same conclusions will emerge. Consider reliability when you make generalizations about your conclusions. Reliability is often tied to the terms *error* and *accuracy*. *Error* is the more general term for whether or not the data or a study area is correct. Error is subdivided into reliability and accuracy. Here, *reliability* still means repeatability. *Accuracy* refers to the precision of a measurement or model. This distinction is clarified with the dartboard example in Figure 11.3. In the left dartboard, each dart is reliability in the same target. It may not be the intended target, but the player can repeat the action. In the right dartboard, the dart has landed on the bull's eye target. Providing that was the intended target, it is accurate. However, for an unskilled dart player, this action is not reliable. For many studies, obtaining reliability and accuracy are difficult because of considerable complexity in

Figure 11.3   The dartboard represents reliability and accuracy. The left dartboard illustrates reliability because on repeated attempts, the dart lands at the correct location. If the desired result is the bull's eye, it is not accurate. The right dartboard, however, illustrates accuracy. One dart landed on the correct location. It is not reliable, however, because subsequent attempts did not.

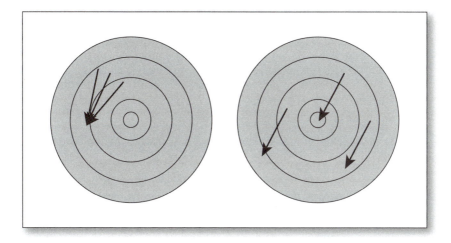

the physical and social world. Nevertheless, it remains a worthwhile tool for proposal evaluation.

A final mechanism for proposal evaluation is the criteria established by major funding agencies such as the National Institutes of Health (NIH) and the National Science Foundation (NSF). These agencies have specific review criteria used by external reviewers and through their internal process. Generally, these criteria include project significance, qualification of the investigators, innovation, approach, and social relevance and impact. These benchmarks are the gauges your advisor and committee will use to evaluate your dissertation proposal.

Activities

By now you should have it in your head that there is quite a bit that goes into describing and evaluating methods for a research proposal. The activities described here will help formulate and evaluate your research methods.

🕐 To Do List

1. Look broadly first. Either alone or with a small group of friends, list as many unique quantitative and then qualitative methods as possible. Aim for a list of about 40 or so for each, which is really just scratching the surface of possible methods. This is an important exercise because it reminds you of all the possible quantitative and qualitative approaches out there. If stumped, go to a research methods book (you probably took such a course as an undergraduate) and look at techniques listed there.

2. Return to your best-of-the-best Roll-a-Research question. Can you use the list you just created to pick out a method that matches this question? If not, why? Is the question not specific enough (weak bridge)? Re-create this question so you can list the methods.

3. From your problem statement, write your own research question or objective here:_____
   _____

4. Identify the pieces that include the method. Which template is better for you?

5. Prepare an outline for the more suited template. Write your methods on this outline.

6. Obtain feedback. Share your methods with your advisor and several of your fellow graduate students.

7. Prepare and present orally your research methods in a 5- to 6-minute presentation. Video yourself if no one is available to listen. Evaluate how effectively you have expressed your ideas.

8. Remember your motivational phrases or images from the first chapter. You are pushing through the hard part of a proposal. Reminder yourself to stay strong.

Reminders

- The methods section describes to the reader how the research will be conducted.
- Consider one of two templates for your methods section or find a template that suits your work better.
  - Study Area, Data, Analysis
  - New Approach, Implementation, Evaluation

- Type I and Type II errors occur when the wrong conclusion is reached.
- *Validity* and *reliability* refer to whether your conclusions are reasonable and whether the study can be repeated.

References

Trochim, W. M. (2006). *The research methods knowledge base* (2nd ed.). Retrieved from www.socialresearchmethods.net/kb

Wentz, E. A., Peuquet D. J., & Anderson, S. (2010). An ensemble approach to space-time interpolation. *International Journal of Geographical Information Science, 24*(9), 1309–1325.

Wentz, E. A., Wills A. J., Kim, W. K., Myint S. W., Gober, P., & Balling, R. C. Jr. (in press). Factors influencing water consumption in multifamily housing in Tempe, AZ. *The Professional Geographer.*

12

Research Proposal

Introduction

Previous chapters describe in detail how to write the content for the major sections of a research proposal. The objective now is to bring those pieces together into a cohesive document: a written research proposal. This culminating activity involves cutting and pasting, rewriting, and new writing. It is a matter of systematically and intelligently bringing the elements you have created together.

Provided here is a generic proposal structure and suggested content that is fairly common among the social and behavior sciences. Since most professors, academic units, and universities have particular guidelines or requirements for proposal structure and content, some adaptation may be required. The organization presented here, however, works for many student research projects. Keep in mind that advisors, committee members, and potentially external reviewers will evaluate the final proposal on clarity, content, *and* whether specified guidelines are met. The following is the content and organization I recommend:

1. A *cover page*, which contains the title, your name, committee member names, and the date

2. An *introduction* to the problem describing the general scope of the project and why it is important

3. A *literature review* synthesizing prior research and describing the theoretical framework of your research

4. *Specific objectives or research questions* and hypotheses (when appropriate) your proposal addresses

5. A detailed description of your *research methods*, including data collection and analytical approaches

6. *Project significance and implications*

7. An annotated *time line* for the anticipated completion of the research

8. An alphabetized list of *references*

9. *Appendix* (optional)

This chapter contains guidelines on the content for each section, parameters to decide how long each section might be, and Action Items describing how to craft and revise the entire document. Several Action Items are embedded in the chapter, as with previous chapters. However, the majority of Action Items appear as a "to do" list at the end of the chapter. The reason for this difference is because I present and describe the contents of the proposal in the order they appear in the final document (as illustrated in the preceding list). Crafting those individual sections, however, requires they be written in a different order, starting with the research methods.

Proposal Content

In the first paragraph of this chapter, I suggested that most of the pieces for the proposal already exist. It appears to be just a matter of bringing them together, and voila, it is done. I wish it were that easy. Remember first that the earlier documents were written as stand-alone pieces. Now they need to be integrated into a cohesive whole. Second, your ideas have matured since you wrote the area of specialization. You have new ideas and a new frame of reference that need to be incorporated. Clearly, both of these reasons suggest revising existing and writing new text. The remainder of this section describes the content for each of the sections of the proposal.

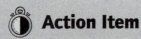

Action Item

Start a new word processing file for your proposal. Using either the organization described earlier or an outline suited best for your project, craft the headings for the proposal sections. As you begin to fill in these sections, pay particular attention to how one section links to another. These transitions need to be overt so the reader knows the logical relationship of your ideas.

TITLE

For each piece from the preceding chapters, you should have written a short title. Hopefully they were more substantive than "Methods for my Project." The title of the proposal is an important piece because it reflects what you consider the essential elements of your research. The title tells outsiders if they should read further, even just the abstract. Titles that are too short may not tell enough. Long titles may be too cumbersome to explain the concept clearly. Balance these with a detailed, clear, and informative title reflecting the emphasis of your work. Try starting with a "working" title, and then after the proposal (or manuscript) is written, evaluate it again. Here is an example of a title in development:

Explaining vulnerability

Explaining vulnerability of adolescent girls

Explaining vulnerability of adolescent girls in North America

Explaining vulnerability of adolescent girls in North America to violence

Explaining vulnerability of adolescent girls in North America to violence through empirical field work

As you can see, each subsequent title offers more specificity. The first title could refer to nearly anything. By the final title, the content of the study is clear, including some indication of the methods. However, while specificity is critical, too much jargon or convolution adds confusion rather than clarity.

 Quick Task

Write several titles and share them with your advisor and fellow students. Ask for feedback. There are also online forums (e.g., http://ismythesishotornot.com) where you can evaluate and receive feedback for thesis statements.

INTRODUCTION

The introduction describes the topic, which should be obvious from the title, and the context for the research you conducted. This section is relatively short but important because it frames the research and provides enough detail so that the literature review (which comes next) does not seem to the reader like detailed content without purpose. Part of your introduction is derived from your area of specialization statement (AOS) from Chapter 4 but includes reference to a small portion of the problem statement from Chapter 10.

First provide a sentence stating the topic. If you recall from the AOS description, the initial statement was direct, something along the lines of "I am a demographer." Do not start your proposal with a general area like you did with the AOS; however, it is appropriate to begin with something specific, such as, "The goal of my proposal is better understand how social networking websites impact online dating." This approach states exactly your plan, leaving the remainder of the proposal to elaborate. Another way to approach the introduction is to begin with a broad statement on the problem context. These statements describe the big picture, such as rising concerns over climate change, biodiversity, economic crisis, or urban poverty. The remainder of the proposal adds specificity on how you plan to fill a gap in this general research area.

The remainder of the introduction elaborates on your research plans. For first sentences that begin with specific goals, subsequent statements place those goals into the big picture through general statements, definitions, and examples. For first sentences that begin with the big picture, subsequent statements need to provide specificity through definitions, examples, and finally specific research objectives. Regardless of your personal organization, the reader needs to know what the proposal is about (the topic) and why it is important to solve (the context).

LITERATURE REVIEW

The literature review is the next logical section after the introduction because it describes in detail how other researchers have addressed this topic. Given that your experience with your topic has matured since you first wrote the literature review, this section of the proposal probably requires more substantial revisions than others. In the first draft, written in Chapter 7, you were likely new to the subject, so coverage of the material was comprehensive. The goal was to show readers you knew the subject area. It was essential that your understanding of the subject and the gaps in the research were fully discussed.

In contrast to a broad literature review, the literature review in the proposal is written to support your specific research objectives or questions. It is written so the reader understands the specific gaps in the knowledge you aim to fill. In some disciplines, the literature review is so tightly bound to the research questions that it is a skeletal form by comparison. Guidance from your advisor is prudent at this stage to ensure you meet the expected requirements. Regardless of its depth, the literature review in the proposal is a synthesis, not a summary, of what is relevant to your research. Review Chapter 7 for clarity on this distinction.

The literature review in the proposal needs an introductory paragraph to transition from the proposal introduction. The introductory paragraph has two primary elements. First, you state the major themes covered in the literature review. Include a brief statement describing the rationale for the why these themes were selected. Second, the introductory paragraph describes the organizing structure of the literature review. As described in Chapter 6 on writing, you need to "tell them what you are going to tell them." Key to maintaining this organization is clear section headings on the subtopics and overt transitions between them.

Readers knowledgeable about the topic and subtopics are likely familiar with the larger literature and need to know that you are too. So while you have focused on literature specific to your research questions or objectives, you will need to point to these minor themes not discussed in detail like your major themes. These minor themes (relative to your research) can be identified with a stop sign in the mind mapping of the literature (see Figure 12.1). Refer to these themes in the literature review with brief statements to acknowledge their existence. They can be referenced generally by stating, "There is research in *such and such* area (REF, REF, REF). They do *this and that*, but it is not related to my topic because of *X and Y*."

The literature review concludes with a paragraph summarizing the literature and identifying the gaps. The summary simplifies what is known about the topics in your field. Statements describing gaps detail broad unknowns you and other investigators can investigate.

RESEARCH OBJECTIVES OR QUESTIONS

Since the end of the literature review describes gaps in the literature, this is a perfect segue to your specific research questions or objectives. In fact, all sections of the proposal are in some way directly linked to this section. The research objectives or questions represent the heart of your project. The introduction describes the goal of the project, the literature review gaps in knowledge about the project, and the methods your approach. All sections pivot around your research objectives or questions directly.

Writing the research question or objective therefore requires careful consideration of all you have written. Much of what is stated in this section is derived from your problem statement described in Chapter 10. It begins with a paragraph describing the gaps to be filled by the proposed research. This is followed by two to five specific research objectives or questions. The last part of this section is several paragraphs describing the intended outcomes (for objectives) or stating the hypotheses (for questions). The section itself is simple and often short, but it is mandatory that it is clear and specific.

METHODS

The methods section provides the roadmap for developing a research project. It is detailed and the substance on which proposals are evaluated. The methods section is perhaps the easiest to translate from the original draft (from Chapter 11) to the final proposal. Nearly the whole thing can be copied directly to the proposal. Feedback received from the original draft may provide guidance on content or structural changes, but unlike the literature review, little needs to be trimmed.

 Action Item

The methods section is the starting point for writing the proposal. It should be pretty fresh in mind so little momentum is lost. Copy this section into the outline you created earlier. Revise the methods by incorporating feedback, trimming unnecessary words, and adding content where possible. Count the words or number of pages as guidance to the overall length of the proposal. Decide now if you need to expand or trim the methods section.

Figure 12.1 This figure shows how mind-mapping software helps organize the content of the literature review into minor and major themes.

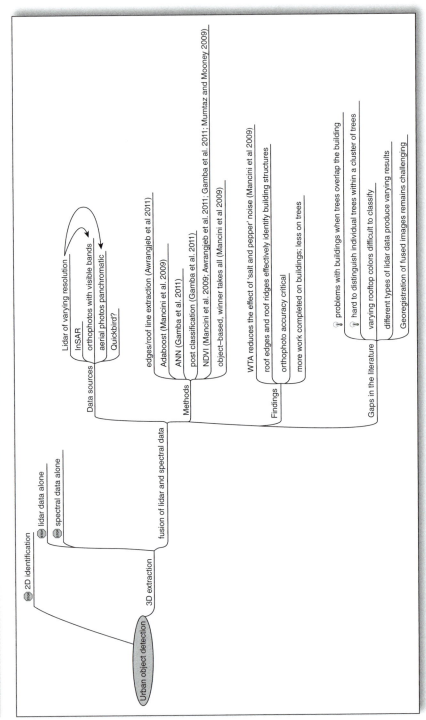

Source: This map was created with Freemind.

ANTICIPATED RESULTS AND PROJECT SIGNIFICANCE

The content of the proposal concludes with what you expect to learn and why the project has merit. Your goal is to convince your evaluators that what you propose contributes to the body of knowledge in a meaningful way. The National Science Foundation requires that proposals identify the contribution to knowledge and merit through two criteria: intellectual merit and broader impacts. *Intellectual merit* refers to the academic reasons for your research (anticipated results). *Broader impacts* are the societal reasons for your research (project significance).

The anticipated results address what you expect to find. The project significance answers why it matters. These questions are addressed in part in the introduction but only in a general sense. Here you explain exactly how the success of your project will lead to better understanding, new insights, a better environment, or a better society. The section itself does not need to be long but needs to say something substantive. This section also serves to summarize or conclude your thoughts.

TIME LINE

After providing the significance, most proposals contain a time line to describe the project from proposal defense to completion. The time line shows the reader you know how to divide the project into specific tasks and how long each task should take to complete. There are two pieces to the time line: a graphic showing when each stage of the project will be undertaken and a paragraph or two annotating the time line. The steps you need to include in both the graphic and annotation may be obvious to you because they were just described in the methods. However, clarification and specificity are essential for a thorough proposal. Figure 12.2 shows an example of a time line graphic, and the paragraph that follows represents a portion of the annotation.

The spring term (months April–June) will be devoted to data collection and assembly. During this time I will start the writing for Topic #1. During the summer and into the fall (July–Oct), I will be conducting the data analysis. During the fall term (Sept–Dec), I will be writing, applying for academic jobs, and attending professional meetings. Throughout the 12-month period, I will be writing on each of my three topics. I plan to defend my dissertation in March of next year.

A time line should be written as *realistically* as possible. In other words, avoid being overly ambitious or overly cautious. Ideally, you want to be done in the most timely manner possible, but unexpected challenges typically arise. Set a time line that includes these unexpected events. Most students have Plan B in their back pocket (typically not part of the proposal) as a fallback. This is important especially to avoid emotional fallout from drifting away from Plan A.

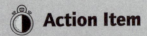

Action Item

Write a time line. The time line needs to be graphic and annotated. The annotation may seem redundant to what is in the graphic, but explanation is important. Notice a few things here in the content of the time line in Figure 12.2, which should apply to most time lines:

a. It is roughly 12 months from proposal defense to dissertation defense.

b. The writing starts immediately; not something saved for the end.

c. There are roughly two to three activities per month and no more.

d. It includes other professional, nondissertation activities such as attending professional meetings and applying for jobs.

REFERENCES

The reference section is critical and needs to be done right. Each previous section likely referred to existing literature. This section identifies where that literature is published. There are many styles for referencing the literature. My recommendation is to pick a style typical to your discipline and be consistent throughout the document. One suggestion is to pick the style from one of the prominent journals in your field. A bibliographic style is required for the dissertation, so it is easiest to begin the habit of accurate referencing now. Software packages can be used to automatically format references into any desired style. Chapters 6 and 7 discuss reference software.

APPENDICES

The content in most appendices for a proposal is preliminary data or results from a pilot study. The proposal itself does not need to contain results, but you may want to demonstrate the potential of your research with work completed so far. This could involve data collection strategies, computer programs, or results. Many successful proposals do not have appendices, so there is no need to worry if yours does not.

Figure 12.2 Sample time line and supporting paragraph for completing a dissertation.

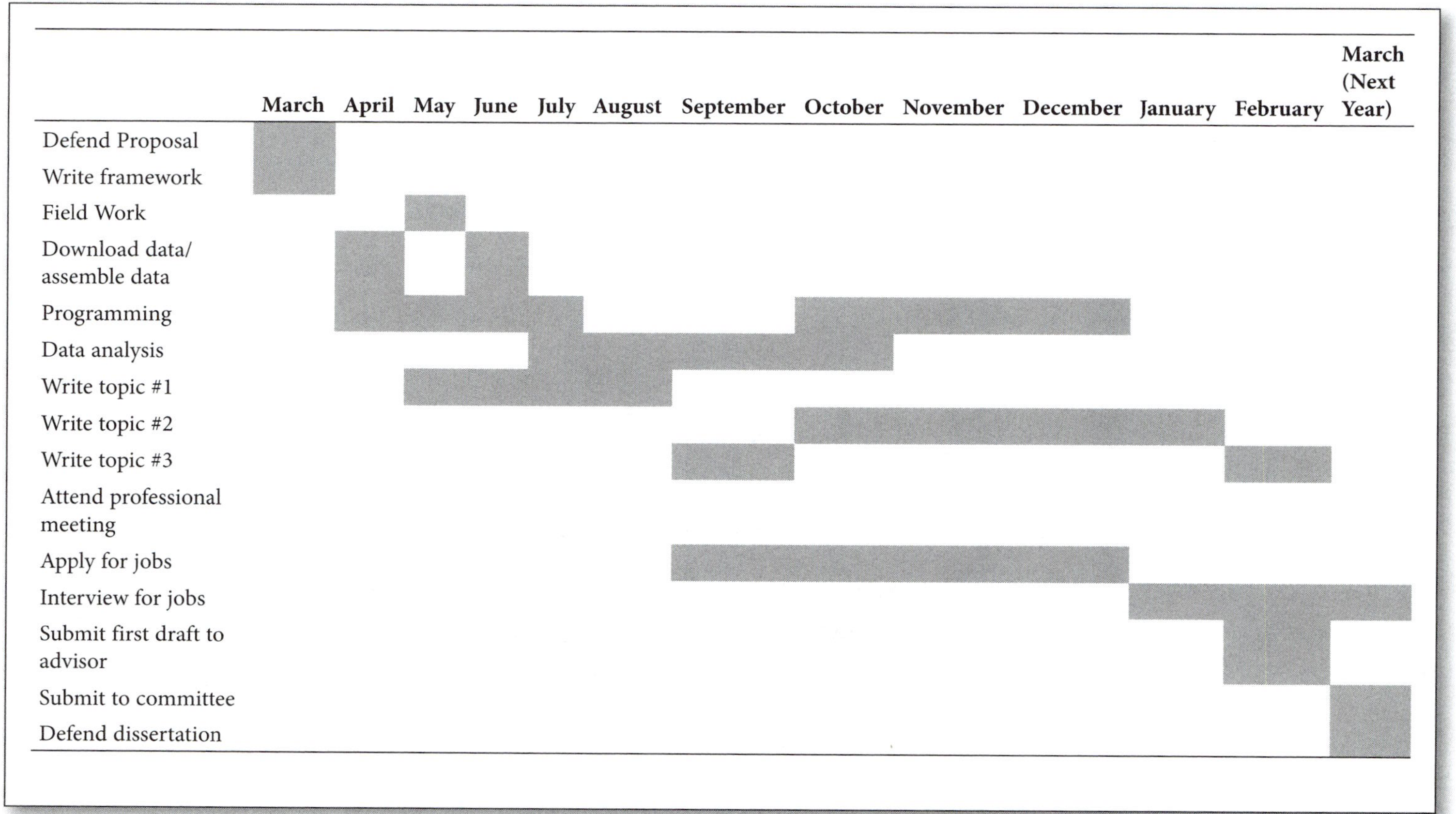

Length and Formatting

"How long does it have to be?"

That question is not reserved for undergraduate students who want to minimize the amount of work ahead. Rather, proposal length provides an indication of the depth level expected by evaluators (graduate committee or funding agency). The length of your proposal (whether counted in pages or total words) depends on the guidelines provided by advisors, departments, graduate colleges, or external funding agencies. Alternatively, there may be no guidelines, expectations, or rules—but it is your responsibility to ask and to know.

Regardless of the length mandated, each section of your proposal should fit into a standard proportioned whole, as illustrated in Figure 12.3. Each of the 15 tick marks (-) shown in Figure 12.3 can represent a certain number of pages. For example, if each tick mark represents two pages of text, then the total number of pages is 30. This means there are two pages for the introduction, eight pages for the literature review, two pages for the research questions, and so on. Notice that the majority of tick marks (six) goes to the methods. This is because the relative amount of depth in the document should emphasize the approach—what you are going to do. More often than not, student dissertation proposals have long literature reviews, perhaps too long.

Figure 12.3 can be translated easily from pages into word count. Word count is an easier metric to quantify content depth because it is independent of formatting (described shortly). Roughly speaking, 280 words translates into a single double-spaced page and 500 words into a single-spaced page. Using word count, the percentage of words per section can be compared to the Table 12.1 template that follows.

Table 12.1 shows the template percentage, the total words from a PhD proposal, and the observed percentage of each section relative to the whole document (excluding appendices). As you can see, comparing the template percentage to the observed percentage, this sample proposal has a good balance in each section. That means that relative to its length, this proposal provides the appropriate amount of depth per section. In fact, these proportions are more realistic (e.g., a slightly larger introduction and a bit less in the research questions and the significance and time line sections) than the template. In printed form, the total document for this sample is about 45 pages, including title page and appendices, which were not counted here.

Proposal formatting refers to document qualities including font type and size, double versus single spacing, page layout, table style, and reference style. Many institutions or academic units and nearly all funding agencies have rules or guidelines on formatting. These rules or guidelines are in place to maintain consistency among a collection of submitted proposals. Institutions and academic units may have more rules or guidelines for the thesis or dissertation

Figure 12.3   Relative proportion of each proposal section to the total length.

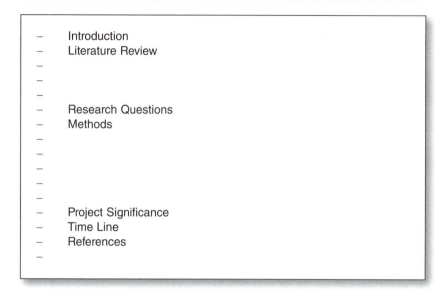

- Introduction
- Literature Review
-
-
-
- Research Questions
- Methods
-
-
-
-
- Project Significance
- Time Line
- References
-

Table 12.1   Template percentages of a recent PhD proposal.

Section	Template percentage (%)	Actual Words	Observed Percentage (%)
Introduction	6.25	999	8.67
Literature Review	25.00	2,916	25.29
Research Questions	6.25	385	3.34
Methods	37.50	4,781	41.47
Project Significance	6.25	232	2.01
Time Line	6.25	147	1.28
References	12.50	2,068	17.94

than for the proposal. For funding agencies, on the other hand, strictness levels the playing field among a group of submitted proposals. This means all proposals competing for funding have the same amount of space to argue their perspective. The total number of pages is not sufficient because font size and page layout, for example, affect the total number of words, giving an unfair advantage to anyone reducing font size and decreasing page margins. To simplify this, many abstract and manuscript submission guidelines are now based on total word count rather than page length.

Proposal Writing Activities

The content, from each of the sections previously written, needs to be evaluated in the context of preparing to write a single document. It is best to start in the middle, work backward to the beginning, and then finish up at the end. Nine simple steps to completion!

🕐 To Do List

The following Action Items are listed in the order I suggest you revise the documents you already have in hand. This is not the order in which they should be presented. The presentation order either reflects that suggested earlier or an agreed-upon order between you and your advisor.

1. The research methods were incorporated into your first draft. Calculate the number of words in this section and compare it to the template in Figure 12.3. This gives you a target for the remainder of the proposal. Are you in line with what your advisor expects? Revise now if necessary.

2. Return to the research questions or objectives you wrote in your problem statement (Chapter 10). Do the methods you wrote indeed answer the questions or objectives as written? Remember that the research questions or objectives are a bridge between the literature review and the methods. Is that bridge still intact? Revise this section by trimming unnecessary words and reducing or eliminating the introduction. Once embedded in the proposal, any introductory material will be redundant and should be removed.

3. Still thinking about the bridge, read the comprehensive literature review as is (avoid revising at first). Read now for content. With the comprehensive literature review in mind, write the last paragraph for your proposal where you summarize the literature and identify gaps. This paragraph should include some moderately focused literature and gaps you do not address in your research questions or objectives.

4. Revise the literature review with the context of the research questions or objectives in mind and the last paragraph from the comprehensive literature review. The literature review in this revision is not comprehensive; all that you know is not included. Instead it is focused on the research or objective you aim to answer or complete.

   • Count the words in your comprehensive literature review. Compare that number to Table 12.1 to determine a target length.

- Identify the key topics of your existing literature review that you need to include in detail to support your research questions.
- Write an outline that structures these topics in a clear and logical order.
- Copy and then revise these sections in the new structure. Be sure you add details where needed and eliminate unnecessary details.
- If you are struggling with the section, return to the skills in Chapter 10 to verify you are synthesizing and not summarizing the literature.

5. The content of introduction is derived from both the problem statement (Chapter 10) introduction you just deleted and from your area-of-specialization statement (Chapter 4). Start by composing the introduction from your AOS statement with broad information—the topic of study and how it is being solved. Then add the content from the problem statement introduction to enhance it with more detail on the problem this research proposal aims to solve.

6. The section on anticipated results and project significance is written after the introduction but is located toward the end of the proposal. This typically short section echoes the introduction by reminding readers why this research matters.

7. Update your references or bibliography. If you do it manually, check and recheck to make sure nothing is missing from your references and that everything in your reference section is cited in your proposal. If you generate references with software, make sure they are correct too because a title entered incorrectly into the software database will appear incorrectly in your reference list too.

8. Include appendices if needed. This can be the results from a pilot study, the survey instruments, or any ancillary information needed to support your proposal.

9. The next important step is to proofread and get feedback.

- Most people read and edit digitally, using very little paper. This is an occasion, however, where reading on paper is needed. So print the whole proposal. Next, read the proposal backward. Okay, not each sentence but each section starting with the references (or appendices if you have them). To a certain extent, you wrote the proposal backward, so read it that way too. When reading the references, look for too much reliance on a single author; evaluate whether the breadth of the literature is represented appropriately; review the formatting of the references. Then go backward section by section. When done, read the whole thing forward. Look for the connections between each section as designed.

(Continued)

(Continued)

- Obtain feedback, as much as possible from your village. Check with your advisor on when to give your proposal to your committee. Some committee members only want to see the submitted proposal; others want to be involved in proposal preparation.
- Revise and proofread it again. I have also found it better to revise it and then set it down for 24 hours before proofreading and revising again. A little bit of time gives you mental distance and lets you read (and evaluate) it more objectively.

Reminders

- Start the whole document by rewriting the methods section.
- Revise the literature review so it is focused on your specific problem.
- Include an annotated time line.
- Describe the project's significance.
- Read, reread, and revise.

13

Oral Presentations

Introduction

The previous chapters describe how to design and write a dissertation proposal. For most programs, the final step in the proposal process is to orally present (and defend) your ideas to your graduate committee. This chapter describes what is required to prepare and deliver an excellent oral presentation. Like writing, learning to present orally is a skill that can be learned. Unfortunately, not everyone learns how to do this.

Just think about a colloquium you attended by a recognized scholar in your field. The "graphics" were a series of bulleted text slides and large data tables. You had difficulty concentrating because you had to both listen to what he or she said while simultaneously reading the text or trying to focus on the data tables. By the middle of the presentation, your mind wandered off and maybe you even had trouble staying awake. By the time the question-and-answer portion of the talk arrived, you were detached from the presentation and could not think of a question to ask. You might have even left the presentation thinking the problem was you; that you just did not know enough to follow what he or she said. More than likely, however, it was not you. And unfortunately for you, there was probably some interesting material covered, but it was unavailable to you and the rest of the audience because of a poorly prepared and delivered presentation.

There is an easy way to avoid being this presenter. It requires knowledge of the subject matter (which the person in the example had) and how to organize and deliver a presentation. Knowledge of the subject matter is easy: You just wrote a 30-plus-page manuscript describing it. Knowing how to select the pieces that go into an oral presentation and delivering it aloud is the next step.

Like the written word, an oral presentation is a story with a beginning, middle, and end. This organization provides you and the audience with an understood structure to share a single message—the take-home idea. In three sections you present the idea, elaborate on the idea, and provide a recapitulation to solidify the idea. This chapter helps you select and organize the content that fits into this structure and craft visual aids that prepare you to deliver an engaging presentation.

Preparation

Early in my career, the thought of giving a presentation gave me anxiety. I would fret over the entire process from preparation to delivery. At some point, I decided I needed to learn to not fret, deliver a well-thought-out presentation, and at least appear to be relaxed about it. I started to observe the common qualities of excellent presentations and incorporate the techniques and style into my own. For example, many years ago at the University of Rhode Island, I presented a paper at a conference along with my colleagues. Unlike my presentation, which was stiff and heavily rehearsed, the presentation by one colleague flowed naturally and engaged the audience. I aspired to that presentation style. Since then, I have had the opportunity to observe and attend numerous excellent presentations and use them as role models.

I now enjoy giving presentations. I aim for an easygoing style, and all goes well providing I am prepared. One lesson learned, however, is that the latter part—preparation—is essential. Preparation means the content is selected and organized, visual aids are prepared, and you practice. This section describes how to minimize anxiety and maximize effectiveness through preparation.

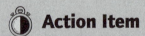 **Action Item**

Think of an excellent presentation you attended. List three or four qualities that made it such. Alternatively or simultaneously, think of a poor presentation you attended. What were some of the characteristics of this presentation?

AUDIENCE

The first step in preparing an academic presentation is identifying the likely audience and knowing the duration of the presentation. Knowing the target audience helps you identify the knowledge level and expectations of the people listening to you. That group could range from the general public, to a general academic audience, a discipline-specific group, or a focused group within your specialty. The duration reflects how much time you are given to speak and suggests a depth level for the content. In thinking about the duration of your presentation, you also need to plan for ample time for questions and answers.

Scholars attend and deliver presentations with varying audiences and durations. These often reflect the attention span of listeners in a particular setting. A summary of these talk types plus their typical audience is listed in Table 13.1. Some presentations, such as those at a conference, are short because conference attendees want to hear from multiple people. Longer presentations, such

Table 13.1   Presentations and their audiences.

Presentation Type	Audience	Duration	Audience Size
Poster	Varies from experts to novices	5 minutes	2–15
Proposal defense	Disciplinary knowledge; some in audience with specific domain knowledge	20–60 minutes depending on the discipline, department, and committee	5–30
Dissertation or thesis defense	Disciplinary knowledge; some in audience with specific domain knowledge	20–60 minutes depending on the discipline, department, and committee	5–30
Lecture for an academic course	Novices	20–180 minutes	20–300
Academic job interview	Disciplinary knowledge with little or no specific domain knowledge	45–60 minutes	20–40
Conference	Disciplinary knowledge with some, little, or no specific domain knowledge	5–45 minutes	20–100
Local public (e.g., Kiwanis or Rotary club)	Little disciplinary knowledge but interested in a wide range of topics	45–60 minutes	15–50
Colloquia	Disciplinary knowledge with little or no specific domain knowledge	45–60 minutes	30–75
Keynote address	Varies from disciplinary knowledge to general science audience	45–60 minutes	75–500+

as a colloquium or keynote address, assume the audience is attending specifically to hear more detail from that person. Rarely do presentations go beyond an hour simply because few people have attention spans that last longer than that. In addition to the academic audience, presentations are also given to local interest groups such as community centers, retirement facilities, and special interest groups.

Regardless of the target audience or the duration of the presentation, your story needs a specific message. The message refers to the take-home idea you want to share with the audience and goes beyond the title or theme of the talk.

While Table 13.1 lists possible audience size, the size of the audience really does not matter. A larger audience will likely have fewer people with domain expertise, which tells you your message needs to be more generalized. Regardless of how many people are in the room or how long the presentation takes, planning requires time and effort.

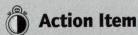 **Action Item**

Plan for your proposal defense. Go to one or more defenses in your unit. Evaluate how long the presentations are and estimate how large the audiences are. Talk with your advisor about the expected duration of your oral presentation.

CONTENT

One challenge with many presentations is trying to include too much content. There seems to be this thought that the audience needs to hear every detail on every piece of the research effort. This could be due to a lack of awareness of how much to include. Alternatively, pride and ego could drive presenters to think the audience needs to know how intelligent they are; the audience needs to see how much they know or have done; or the audience can't possible understand everything without all the detail.

An effective presentation is not about describing everything. Instead, presenters need to remember the goal is to explain one take-home message and do that well. Listening to a presentation is a passive activity. This means it is more difficult for listeners to engage and comprehend material compared to active participation (which happens when someone is reading or writing). Engaging with the audience and keeping them interested is the responsibility of the presenter, not the listener. That said, the audience needs material presented in small doses, slowly, and with pauses. Examples and visual graphics help too.

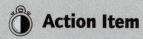

Action Item

Create a flowchart of your approach or methods. This graphic serves to streamline the content of your proposal and identify the primary take-home message of your oral presentation. You may want to include this graphic in your presentation.

ORGANIZATION

The structure of the presentation or the order in which ideas are presented is stated in the introduction of this chapter but now needs more elaboration. The structure is to tell the audience what you are going to tell them; tell them; and tell them what you told them. In a short presentation, this organization needs to be tight and concise. In longer presentations, this organization is mandatory to keep the audience in tune with the presentation. This section guides you through some specifics on how to do this—specifically for a dissertation defense.

The material in the oral presentation has a similar order and content to the written document. Using the same structure as the written proposal, the order could be the following:

Introduction

Literature Review

Research Question(s)

Methods

Time Line

The difference between the written word and oral presentation for a proposal is which section receives the most emphasis. In the oral presentation, the take-home message is the methods that will answer a research question. The introduction and literature review together serve as the "tell them what this is about" section, and the time line serves as the "tell them what you told them" section. The amount of time spent on the first and the last sections is short compared to the "tell them" section. The breakdown on time spent on each section could be the following:

Introduction   4 minutes

Literature Review   3 minutes

Research Question   2 minutes

Methods   15 minutes

Time Line   2 minutes

This organization and allotted time results in a 26-minute presentation with a strong emphasis on the methods section. After all, the audience cares most about what you are going to do. Other details that may be included (e.g., pilot study results) can be worked into this structure, but the emphasis on your methods needs to be retained. A common mistake is students dedicating too much time and detail on the literature review; after all, you have learned a lot about what other people have done. This is a mistake though because the take-home message is what you are going to do to earn your degree.

 Action Item

Using the organization of your proposal, write the outline. Identify how many minutes you aim to devote to each section. The balance should emphasize the methods over other sections.

VISUAL AIDS

Visual aids are shared with the audience through handouts, physical examples, or, most commonly, images displayed on a large screen. Any visual aid helps the presenter explain concepts. The shared images, often created using software such as PowerPoint, help the presenter keep a presentation focused and on task. Visual aids help the audience better comprehend the talk because of key illustrations. That said, the three best colloquia I ever attended were delivered without a single visual aid. The speaker stood in front of the audience (in one case, with notes) and delivered a well-organized presentation. The audience was engaged and listened to the speaker the entire time. So while visual aids help, they are not mandatory. The reason they help can be explained through one famous Confucius quote that reads,

I hear and I forget. I see and I remember. I do and I understand.

As the Confucius quote suggests, people learn best by doing, seeing is second best, and hearing alone remains better than nothing. The goal of using visual aids is to help the audience to remember or—even better—to understand your message. Because the most common type of visual aid used in presentations is the shared image, the remaining comments focus on this type.

Most speakers rely on shared images to support the presentation. In poor presentations, images are used as a crutch for the speaker rather than as an aid to the listener. When developing shared images, decide if they assist the listener by adding interest and information the verbal descriptions do not or perhaps provide a framework for the presentation.

The general rule of thumb for preparing a presentation is one slide per minute of presentation time. This is an average time per slide because the natural flow of the presentation will require more time for some slides and less for others. Over the years, this guideline has proved reliable. Erring on too few slides is better than erring on too many. A poorly executed presentation is when an author skips through several slides and barges to the end because of limited time. In the end, the audience may feel cheated and respect for the speaker may diminish.

A second rule of thumb refers to the text-only slide. A text-only side contains a title and list of bulleted sentences, phrases, or words. Too much text on slides leads to a poor presentation. The advice is universal: minimize the amount of text on slides. For example, a 45-minute talk that allows 15 minutes for questions can be effective with approximately 35 slides (slightly less than the one slide per minute rule) featuring 70 total words. This is an average of two words per slide. Since some slides (e.g., the title slide) typically have more words, some slides will show only graphics or pictures.

The reason too much text on slides is problematic is because when a text slide is shown, the audience attempts to read it. When the speaker is talking, the audience is trying to read and listen at the same time, which is difficult. In the end, the audience has neither read nor listened effectively and is therefore weakly informed. As a speaker, if you decide to read the text from the slide instead of speaking, then why have the slide in the first place? If you let the audience read the slide themselves, then why are you there to speak?

A good guideline is that only 10% of the total number of slides should be text only. Using this rule of thumb with the guideline of one slide per minute means there should be only three text slides for a 25-minute (hence 25-slide) presentation. Table 13.2 shows how that might break down using the earlier outline.

This planning leaves a lot of space for nontext slides! Slides with graphics provide additional information beyond words. The methods overview can be presented as a flowchart instead of a list. The time line can be a graphic instead of words. Some more ideas other than bulleted text slides are the following:

Maps showing the study area

Photographs of the study area

Photographs of the data collection equipment

Tables showing data sources and variables

Venn diagram showing the relationship between ideas

Table 13.2   Sample order of presentation slides.

General Topic	Minutes	Slide Topic	Slide Type	Specific Content
Introduction	4	1. Title slide	Title format	
		2. Problem statement	Graphic	
		3. Importance	Graphic	
		4. General research goals	Graphic	
Literature review	3	5. Overview	Graphic	
		6. Topic #1	Graphic	
		7. Topic #2	Graphic	
Research question	2	8. Specific research question	Text	
Methods	15	9. Overview	Graphic	
		10. Study area	Graphic	
		11. Data overview	Graphic	
		12. Data specific	Graphic	
		13. Data specific	Graphic	
		14. Analysis overview	Graphic	
		15. Analysis specific	Graphic	
		16. Analysis specific	Graphic	
		17. Analysis specific	Graphic	
		18. Analysis specific	Graphic	
		19. Analysis specific	Graphic	
		20. Analysis specific	Graphic	
		21. Analysis specific	Graphic	
		22. Analysis specific	Graphic	
		23. Analysis specific	Graphic	
Time line	2	24. Summary	Text	
		25. Time line	Graphic	
		26. Questions?	Graphic	

Some of these nonbulleted slides contain text, such as the Venn diagram. The advantage of this type of "text" slide is that it shows the relationship between the text—not just a list of words. It is therefore acceptable to have small amounts of text on a "graphics" slide.

Without the bulleted text slides for "notes," students fear they will forget what they need to say. They often ask if they can or should read from notes or simply speak without them. My recommendation is to use the method that makes you most comfortable. There are good presentations read verbatim from notes—and also poor ones. Similarly, there are excellent presentations from speakers not using notes—and also poor ones.

 Action Item

Using Table 13.2, fill in the specific content for each slide. Your written proposal will guide your content. Note that, except for the methods, there is little space for excessive details.

SAMPLE PRESENTATION

Figure 13.1 (a–c) shows 15 visual aids for a 15-minute presentation on how to give a presentation. It shows both what not to do (e.g., repeated text-only slides) and what to do (e.g., use of graphic slides). The caption for each figure describes the role each slide contributes to the overall message of the presentation.

Speaking

After effective slides, the second important part of the presentation is the oral delivery of the message. The goal is to use a clear and steady voice using the power of language to command authority. Two things make this happen: confidence and experience. *Confidence* refers to believing you are the expert on the subject and that the audience is there to learn from you. Remember, you are and they are. Experience comes from multiple opportunities to speak. At this point, you may not have years of experience, but you can still practice. This gives you experience too.

Figure 13.1a The first six slides of this presentation represent common visual aids in oral presentations. They contain text—or notes to the author—on the content of the presentation.

Oral Presentations: best practices

Elizabeth A. Wentz
Professor
School of Geographical Sciences and Urban Planning
Arizona State University

Presentation Outline

- Why oral presentations?
- Types of presentations
- Preparing a presentation
  - Content
  - Visual aids
- Presentation day
- Final tips

A word (or two) on presentations

- Plan for the amount of time you have to present
- Prepare notes on what to say for each slide
- Practice your presentation alone
- Practice the presentation with an audience

Level of depth (length of talk)

- Prepare about 1 slide per minute of the presentation
  - For a 40 minute presentation – no more than 40 slides
  - For a 20 minute presentation – no more than 20 slides
- Have a key point in a mind
- Avoid bringing in too much information

Language

- The word "data" is plural, so say "data are" and "these data"
- Avoid jargon
- Do not use informal language such as "and stuff like that"
- Do not use profanity or other foul language

Slide style

- Text slides look like this one – a list of bulleted points
- The problem with these in that they represent "notes" to the speaker
- They are not information to the listener
- What happens is that the audience is unsure whether to listen or to read
- What happens is that they do neither very well
- The result:

>> A poor presentation

Figure 13.1b   The next six slides of the presentation show types of visualizations, including maps, graphs, and time lines. Slides 3 and 4 illustrate how to improve a graphic taken from a computer screen. Slide 3 is a simple screen snapshot and includes too much of the software, which is distracting to the audience. Slide 4 removes the software components and focuses just on the map. Slides 5 and 6 show how to improve tables to more effectively report on research findings.

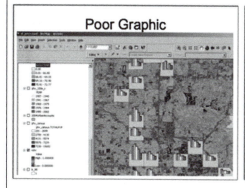

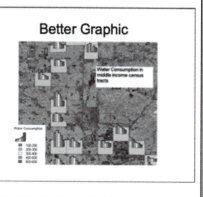

Figure 13.1c   The second-to-last slide discusses how ineffective it is to have too many slides for a presentation. The basic rule of one slide per minute is typically on target. Too many slides force the speaker to rush or to skip to the end of the presentation. The last slide of the presentation is the conclusion and opens up the presentation to the audience for questions.

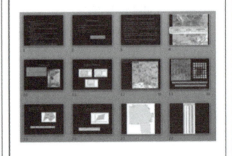

CONFIDENCE

Gaining confidence and having experience are interlinked, but there are tips to make you believe in yourself (or appear to) even before having the extended experience. The first tip is to begin each slide by talking about its graphic. Explain what the audience is seeing and why you have included it in the presentation. It is disconcerting to listen to a person speak and not understand how their words tie to the image on the screen. Connect your words to the graphics.

The second tip is to look at your audience. Another way to put this is to make eye contact. This suggestion is often overlooked when bulleted text slides dominate because the speaker will turn to the screen to read the text and hence look away from the audience. Instead, a presentation with graphic visual aids encourages the speaker to glance at the screen to identify key pieces and then turn back to the audience. Engagement with the audience increases if the lights remain on or partially on. This gives you the opportunity to see the audience and the audience the opportunity to see you. It might seem tempting to retreat into a dark room as a disembodied voice, but the result is a less engaged, less dynamic, and less effective presentation.

A third tip is to learn to speak slowly. This is particularly important when covering vital parts of your presentation. In the case of a research proposal, this means the research question. I advise my students to present the research question in text (no graphics), to read it directly from the slide, and then to pause. The pause (e.g., counting to three) gives the audience the chance to think about the research question—vital to the rest of the talk. Pauses such as this are good for the audience and demonstrate confidence.

A fourth tip is to be selective of your word choices throughout the presentation. Words that are too complex, specific to the subdiscipline, or jargon make the presentation difficult to follow. Also avoid using slang and inappropriate language, which may offend the audience. Match your word choices to your personality, whether that includes jokes or not. Finally, eliminate all apologies. Anything you might want to apologize for, such as poor graphics, going on too long, or excessive details, should have been corrected during preparation.

A final tip for appearing confident is to be aware of your body language. Avoid pacing, fidgeting, or playing with your clothes or a nearby pencil. To minimize these distractions, glance at the ground and identify a small space where you can move comfortably. Dress comfortably but appropriately for the presentation.

EXPERIENCE

Practice is clearly central to being effective and can be accomplished alone or with a small but critical audience.

Alone

Believe it or not, practicing alone can be harder than practicing with an audience. In part it is because you may feel silly standing and talking to yourself. For example, I mumble through sentences, say weird offhand comments, and use awkward hand gestures. Ideally for me, these oddities disappear with an audience! However, after practicing alone, speaking in front of an audience is immensely easier. It is therefore worth the effort to embarrass yourself alone so you do not do the same in front of an audience.

Practicing alone requires standing by the computer (not sitting), speaking aloud (practicing in your head is ineffective), and timing the talk. Standing separates practicing from preparing the talk. In both cases, you are likely in front of a computer. When you prepared the slides, you probably thought about what you would say. Standing and speaking forces you to actually decide on sentences, not just ideas. Speaking aloud instead of practicing in your head also forces you to decide on the order of ideas. In-the-head thoughts run smoothly. Saying them aloud forces you to decide exactly what words to say. Timing yourself has two effects. First, you learn how much (more or less) you have to say during the actual presentation. Second, and more important, it forces you to keep talking during the practice presentation instead of starting over or skipping sections.

As you practice, you will notice strong and weak sections. While giving yourself a pat on the back for the strong sections, also decide what makes them strong. Why did you know more about what to say? Likewise, pay close attention to slides that bring out the "umms" and other distractions. In other words, identify those where you have no idea what you plan to say. At the end of the practice talk return to those slides and write out two to three sentences for them. Say those aloud so the next time you practice, you have solid ideas on what to say. Consider too whether you need to change or eliminate those slides.

After you are done, note the time. Were you too long, too short, or just right? Now is the time to return to edit mode and decide what changes are needed. You might decide that ideas jump too quickly from one slide to the next so you need a transition slide. Alternatively, you may decide that one slide is too similar to another and needs to be deleted. Avoid being too fixed on your presentation. Rearrange the slides and try again. It may be worse, it may be better—and you have learned something.

A Critical Audience

Select a small group (e.g., two or three people) who will provide honest feedback on both the content and delivery of the presentation. At this point, you want to hear the honest truth, even and especially when it is critical. Your goal is to hear the ugly truth so you can improve on your efforts. In addition to the small group, you can record the presentation, so you can review your strengths and weaknesses yourself. The practice of recording a presentation is more effective with an audience than alone. Watching yourself give an oral presentation is one of the more difficult, humbling, and embarrassing things you can do. I promise you this: You will be more critical than any other person you invite.

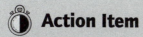

Action Item

Gather a group to practice presenting research. This is particularly effective a few weeks prior to a regional or national conference where students are presenting. Set aside an afternoon (an empty slot during the colloquium is usually available for most people) so that everyone can practice his or her presentation. Find a seminar room and make it official. Invite faculty and other students to attend.

Presentation Day

Getting over the terror of standing up and talking for the most part requires practice and time. You may be feeling anxious, nervous, jittery, and excited all at the same time. All of these emotions are normal. If you are prepared, there is no reason to be nervous. That said, even experienced speakers have butterflies in their stomach from time to time.

Moving past those butterflies and becoming, or at least appearing, relaxed often requires just starting to speak. Move past those first few moments by memorizing the first two to three sentences of the presentation. Once you have started to speak, the practice you did will kick in and you will be confident with your material. The key is simply getting started.

Another tip to overcome presentation anxieties is to arrive early. This will help you know:

how to operate the audio-visual equipment,

how the room looks,

where to stand,

where the computer cables run along the floor (to avoid tripping), and

how to dim and raise the lights.

Finally, on presentation day, remember the importance of oral presentations. In addition to the writing process, an oral presentation disseminates your research. Here are just some reasons to present orally:

to clarify your ideas in a meaningful way

to understand how people interpret your work

to give authority to your work (Kamler & Thomson, 2006)

to defend your position publically

The spoken word is a unique medium for transmitting ideas. Like the written word, it is a linear progression of ideas. But unlike the written word, it is fleeting. Once spoken, the audience does not have the opportunity to rewind and listen again. It is therefore the responsibility of the speaker to deliver the message in small, easily understood doses. Even an intelligent and expert audience appreciates a presentation that lays out the material carefully and slowly.

 Action Item

Watch excellent speakers on the Internet. One example is the David McCandless Ted Talk on data visualization.

Prepare and present an oral presentation of your dissertation proposal. This presentation should be about 20 minutes long and include some parts of the entire proposal, as written in Chapter 12. The proportion, however, is different from the written document. The majority of the slides should describe your method. Use the rule of thumb of one slide per minute of presentation. Furthermore, use bulleted text-only slides sparingly.

Reminders

- Focus on the content; remember the take-home message.
- You are the expert.
- Use only a few text-only slides in the entire presentation.
- Practice: stand up and speak aloud to an audience.
- Leave time for Q & A.

Reference

Kamler, B., & Thomson, P. (2006). *Helping doctoral students write: Pedagogies for supervision.* New York: Routledge.

14

Next Steps

Introduction

Now it is time now to breathe a sigh of relief. Yes, you're done with your proposal. Whew. However . . . while this important hurdle may be complete, it represents only the beginning of a lifelong journey. Compare this lifelong journey to that of a marathon runner. There are two types of marathon runners: those training and preparing for a specific event and those who are always training and conditioning. Those who train for a specific event focus on that event, and nothing stops them from that focus. But when the event is over, they say, "Now I'll do the dishes, see friends, get some work done." In contrast, the other marathoner integrates training and conditioning (even with an upcoming event) into the fabric of normal life. The training and the event are simply a part of life.

The same is true with research. There are focused events (e.g., proposal deadline) that require extra time and effort as the deadline approaches. Just like training for a marathon, proposing and conducting research is not completed as an all-nighter or a weekend sprint. Research too can be embedded into the fabric of everyday life, much like the second type of marathoner. The last chapter of this book discusses the next event, the dissertation research.

One hard lesson in graduate school is the realization that you are no longer an undergraduate, with undergraduate expectations. As an undergraduate, you earn a degree by steadily taking the necessary courses and eventually you get there. It is a matter of "serving time." In contrast, as a graduate student, you take certain classes, but at the end the dissertation or thesis remains a mandatory requirement for earning a degree. It is no longer a matter of serving time but instead of producing something original.

The proposal is a plan toward producing your dissertation and earning your degree. The goal now is to use the plan to your advantage to make things happen. The best way to do this is to think of your proposal as a first (incomplete) draft of your dissertation. This chapter launches you into the next phase of the PhD program: doing the research and writing your dissertation. To do this you can use the proposal for funding applications, learn new tools, write and stick to a time line, participate in the review process, deal with common struggles, and create a recipe for success.

Reuse Your Proposal

The dissertation proposal can serve multiple postproposal defense functions. Three common functions are for funding, first drafts, and time lines. The material in your dissertation proposal is valuable to forward these efforts toward earning your degree.

The activities in this section suggest reusing some of the work already written. This suggests self-plagiarism, which is considered just as unethical as plagiarizing other people's work. The difference here is that the proposal at the moment is unpublished. Once the work moves from a proposal into a published manuscript, the material cannot be reused. Sections with similar content from one manuscript to another, such as the introduction and methods, need to be rewritten for each publication.

FUNDING

Graduate students can find many local and national opportunities for funding to support their dissertation research. Local opportunities may come from department support, such as small travel grants or scholarships for fieldwork. While something small like a travel grant may appear insignificant, the opportunity it provides for professional contacts is essential. Another local source may be the university. Universities often have competitive programs for fellowships so advanced PhD students can focus on writing and not worry about teaching assistantships. In addition to local sources, many prominent public national agencies and private foundations provide graduate student dissertation support. For example, the National Science Foundation (NSF) requests proposals for the dissertation improvement grant program. In addition to the financial support the grant provides, the process gives students experience with grant writing and begins a track record for obtaining external funding.

The dissertation proposal you wrote can be mined for content and reused for these funding applications. In particular, you can use the introduction to define the problem and the methods to describe what you plan to do. However, the amount of the proposal you use depends mostly on the guidelines in the request for proposals (RFP). Granting agencies (even local ones) will describe in detail what needs to be included and how long the application can be. In addition, each grant may focus on a specific part of your dissertation work, not the entire effort. Your goal is to pay clear attention to the requirements needed for each application and use what you can from your existing proposal.

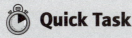

Quick Task

Be proactive about funding options and begin your search immediately, perhaps even before you have defended your proposal. Pay careful attention to application requirements, deadlines, and page limits.

FIRST DRAFTS

Dissertation styles vary, although they tend to be in one of two formats: monograph or multiple paper. A monograph is stylistically like a book because it is crafted as a single document. The advantage of the monograph is that the student has undertaken an in-depth study on a single topic. Subsequently, many students are able to publish their dissertation as a book. The disadvantage is for students who want to publish separate papers from the dissertation because now the single document needs to be divided into separate papers and rewritten.

The alternative to the monograph is to write a multiple-paper style dissertation. This dissertation is written as separate papers that can be published as standalone articles. To provide an overarching structure, often an introduction and conclusion chapter tie together the separate papers. The advantage is that the dissertation has ready-to-submit (or already submitted) manuscripts. Students learn the process of journal article preparation, submission, and revision by participating in the activities as graduate students.

The proposal described in this book is easily extendable to either the monograph or multiple-paper dissertation styles. Returning to the diagram in Chapter 6 on writing, Figure 14.1 illustrates one possible organization of monograph-style dissertation chapters and how they relate to one another. The proposal you just wrote is the first draft of Sections I, II, and III of the dissertation. Key to the subsequent sections is tying the information back to these three sections. The results are an "answer" to the methods; they illustrate what you said you did. The discussion is the answer to the literature review; it describes how your results (previous section) have filled a gap in the literature. The conclusion chapter speaks back to the introduction; the conclusions speak more broadly (back up the spiral) to place your specific contribution back into the context of the general problem.

Separating the proposal into chapters of a multiple-paper style dissertation is similar. The introduction and literature review may be weaved together to form the first draft of Chapter 1 of the dissertation, the overview of the papers. Each of the individual papers (whether there are three, four, or five . . .) need

Figure 14.1   A possible organization of the dissertation chapters and how the content relates to other topics both forward and backward.

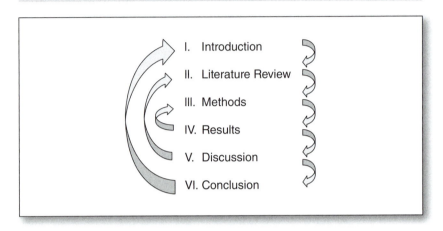

the methods described, which should be included in the Methods section of your dissertation. Likewise, the introductory material for each of the papers can be drafted from the introduction of the proposal.

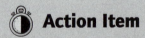 **Action Item**

Create an outline of your dissertation chapters using either the monograph or multiple-paper organization or an alternative. Extract sections from your proposal to begin drafts of your dissertation.

TIME LINE

The time line you wrote for your proposal can be reused to keep you on track toward finishing your degree. One of the biggest struggles graduate students face is staying on schedule. Locke et al. (2007) note that few research projects stay on time. It is unfortunate but true. How do you become the exception and not the rule?

Four tips emerge from your time line to help you stay on track. The first is to avoid overscheduling yourself. This means including only two or three major areas of focus over the course of a week or so. Some of these tasks include teaching or research assistantships, grant or job applications, data entry or analysis, and writing on a particular chapter. The days move quickly, and if you have too many items on your plate, none of these items receive enough of your attention. You are much more effective and efficient if you can pick up where you left off the day before rather than figuring out where you were a week ago or more. Use day-to-day momentum to stay on track.

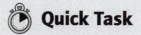

Quick Task

Look critically at your time line. Are there months where you have identified more than three items you need to complete? Is that realistic?

The second tip to staying on track is to plan for unexpected events. Data collection does not go as planned and needs to be redone; analysis you thought would be straightforward is not; your advisor moves to a different university; your computer crashes; you are invited to a research conference, and it is just such a great opportunity. There are hundreds of possible reasons why delays occur. The best way to address them is to have extra padding in the schedule. If you think something will take you about 2 weeks, plan for 4. A rule of thumb is to double the time you think it will take for something to be finished. Even then, you may be off schedule. It is hard staying on track because some of your work depends on other people (who have their own delays).

The third tip to help keep you on track is to learn skills to support your research. One of the more frustrating moments in completing a dissertation is to discover that you do not have the skills to complete a task. This can put you in a panic because you realize that taking the time to learn software, for example, will start to shift the schedule off track from the time line. The goal is to learn what you need before this happens. Some of the needed skills include learning new methods for data collection, using tools for data analysis, and mastering software for creating figures. Make sure that learning the necessary skills is incorporated into your time line.

A fourth tip to maintain your time line is to set a daily schedule, set weekly goals, and regularly revisit long-term goals. You need to be capable of seeing the relationship between the trees (the daily and weekly goals) as well as the forest (the long-term goals). It is easy to get caught up in daily minutia that does not build toward the bigger picture. Prioritize time toward doing small things every day that support long-term goals. It is too easy to check off small short-term tasks when that massive to-do item (the dissertation) looms. Keeping a consistent schedule that includes time for unexpected events involves being adaptive. Long gone are the days when you attended classes and knew weekly what assignments were due. Now the daily and weekly schedules are much more open. It is your responsibility to determine what tasks need to be accomplished each day and by the end of the week. Keep to the daily schedule but add flexibility to accommodate the unexpected—doctor's appointments, car breakdowns, and unplanned meetings with your advisor. To sustain a rigorous work schedule, also include "me time" for exercise and recreation, important for earning the degree but also for the long-term push if you are on an academic career path toward tenure and promotions.

Finally, avoid having a simple phrase such as "do dissertation" on your to-do list. This is why you wrote a time line in the first place, to help you organize your work into manageable pieces. You may think such a phrase would be inspirational and keep you focused. In fact, the opposite is usually true. It may paralyze you because you do not have the smaller pieces you need to build up to "do dissertation." Once you figure out that little pieces build up the whole, you are well on your way.

 ## Action Item

Review the time line you included in your dissertation. Look ahead about 3 months and identify a tangible goal at that point. Working backward from that goal, add detail to your time line to meet that objective. Examine the list (among the other things you said you would do) for feasibility. Answer whether these things can be realistically completed in the time allotted.

 ## Action Item

Avoid at least one of the potential pitfalls by focusing on learning new techniques. Identify and learn new software or programming tools you need to be productive. This could be anything as basic as bibliographic software or a drawing package to as sophisticated as an advanced programming language. Do it now instead of waiting until you feel an immediate deadline pressing.

The Review Process

Throughout this book I suggest you obtain feedback on your ideas, writing, and presentations. Feedback provides you with the opportunity to change the course of your work because of insights and knowledge from supervisors and peers. I have emphasized that providing feedback to other graduate students is also informative and builds skills you can use later in your career. A good opportunity now is to hone these skills by reviewing manuscripts that have been submitted for possible publication in a peer-reviewed journal.

Manuscript reviews have four basic sections: summary, strengths, weaknesses, and recommendation (see Figure 14.2). The section on strengths is often short because you can make blanket and overarching statements. Authors only need to nod and thank you for responding. The section on weaknesses needs to be more detailed. It can be subdivided into major and minor issues and should address how to improve the manuscript or provide detailed reasons why it should not be published (or funded in the case of a grant application review). Finally, there needs to be an explicit statement on whether the manuscript is recommended for publication (or funding). In the recommendation, you can qualify it by stating "as is" or "after minor or major revision." The sections on strengths and weaknesses may seem like sufficient evidence of your opinion, but you still need to be explicit.

Stick to this organization (or something similar) to demonstrate that your review is intended to improve the manuscript, not just criticize it.

In addition to these general guidelines, many journals have specific review criteria. Some include an evaluation of the abstract, tables and figures, writing style, and scientific contribution the manuscript makes to the literature. Carefully examine the review criteria and answer each section honestly and thoroughly.

Figure 14.2.   Outline for a typical manuscript review.

I. A summary of the manuscript; what is the goal?

II. Strengths

III. Weaknesses
   A. Major weaknesses
   B. Minor weaknesses

IV. Recommendation

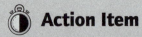

Action Item

1. Ask your advisor or another faculty member to participate in the review process. With the permission of the editor, review a manuscript along with him or her. Be sure to ask your advisor or faculty mentor for any reviewer guidelines the journal provides. Your review along with that of the advisor or faculty mentor can be returned to the editor.

2. Ask your advisor or another faculty member to see the reviews written on a manuscript he or she has submitted for publication. Examine how your advisor responded to each reviewer comment in the revised manuscript.

Recipe for Success

The acronym *ABD* is a relatively common expression referring to PhD candidates who have completed "all but dissertation" in their degree program. Often, the more official term is *PhD candidate* (although it varies by university). There are two types of ABDs: those who finish and those who do not. The goal of course is to be one who finishes. The characteristics of ABDs who complete their PhD degree are intelligence, emotional maturity, and motivation.

Intelligence refers to the cognitive skills or simply the brainpower to do the necessary work. Sometimes students feel insecure about their intelligence because, in all truthfulness, when you are in graduate school you are likely surrounded by other people who are quite bright. Even so, I can honestly say that every single student who has passed a dissertation defense has the intelligence to complete a dissertation. This means you are smart enough to do the work necessary to earn the degree. Avoid letting insecurities about your personal intelligence paralyze you from completing the work.

Emotional maturity refers mostly to being capable of taking the hits (those unplanned events) and moving past them. Students lacking the stability to deal with minor (or major) crises suffer because these issues overtake their ability to focus and continue to work. Some common emotional burdens are boredom, procrastination, anxiety, and uncertainty. These emotions are dangerous and can slow or even stop you from making progress. The best remedy is to stop and analyze the source of the problem. Only then can you address it one little piece at a time. What you may find is that you have become overly emotional about the problem and have simply blown it out of proportion.

For example, perhaps you find yourself procrastinating on the data analysis. Avoiding tasks does not mean you do not have to do them. Each day you find reasons not to do the data analysis. You may look deeper and discover the reason you are avoiding it is because you will need to spend time learning software you have never used before. Yes, studying the help pages and working through tutorials seems like it is taking time away from "real progress" on the dissertation, but in reality it is moving you toward finishing the dissertation. For some students, when moving past obstacles like this becomes impossible, counseling services offered by the university can help provide stability.

The last characteristic is simply motivation. Motivation is a psychological characteristic of people driven to complete an objective or goal. The student who is motivated to finish the PhD will do so regardless of the physical, economic, and psychological barriers. Motivation comes in waves or is steadily there throughout the degree. Different things motivate people differently. Some common motivations are your career and personal, family, or economic pressure. Regardless of the external motivation, what most drives this characteristic is internal motivation—wanting to finish the degree more than anything else. This results in a willingness to dedicate yourself to doing the hard work.

 Action Item

Go to dissertation defenses of your fellow students. Learn to understand the process and visualize yourself doing the same thing. Remember your village.

Remaining Thoughts

Successfully defending your dissertation is a powerful and emotional experience. Chapter 1 describes motivational tools such as images or expressions to keep you on track. One I mentioned earlier is the attitude of a person who trains and competes in a 26.2-mile marathon. There are those who train and participate in a single event and those who make training their life habit. Being the latter, you need to understand that the push to the single event is now past, but the training for the next event continues. Writing and defending the dissertation requires the same focus and dedication as finishing the proposal.

So while events such as the proposal defense are a success, there is always another goal to reach. As speakers at graduation commencements often say, "Continue to learn and continue to seek new knowledge."

> ## 🕐 Quick Task
>
> Revisit or remake the motivational sign or image you created in Chapter 1. Use this to support yourself during the frustrating times of dissertation work.

Last Reminders

- Start the first draft of your dissertation now.
- Learn new tools.
- Add extra time to your time line to plan for the unexpected.
- Assess and overcome emotional burdens.
- Make the decision to finish.

Reference

Locke, L., Spirdusa, W. W., & Silverman, S. J. (2007). *Proposals that work: A guide for planning dissertations and grant proposals.* Thousand Oaks, CA: Sage.

Index

Note: In page references, f indicates figures and t indicates tables.

⑤SAGE research**methods**

The essential online tool for researchers from the world's leading methods publisher

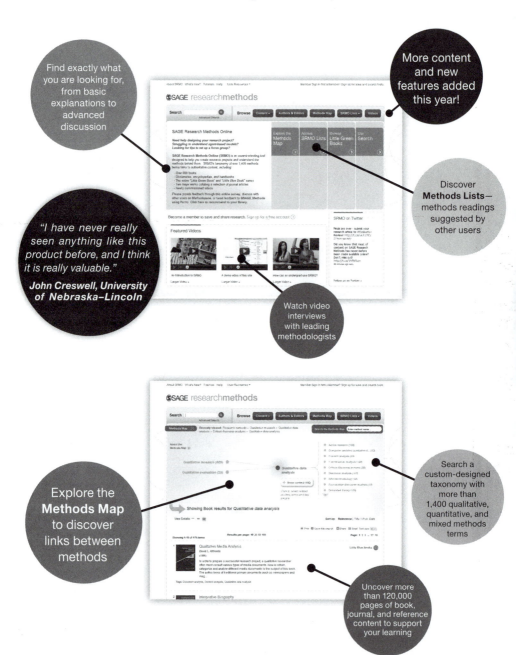

Find exactly what you are looking for, from basic explanations to advanced discussion

More content and new features added this year!

Discover Methods Lists—methods readings suggested by other users

"I have never really seen anything like this product before, and I think it is really valuable."

John Creswell, University of Nebraska–Lincoln

Watch video interviews with leading methodologists

Explore the Methods Map to discover links between methods

Search a custom-designed taxonomy with more than 1,400 qualitative, quantitative, and mixed methods terms

Uncover more than 120,000 pages of book, journal, and reference content to support your learning

Find out more at
www.sageresearchmethods.com